MYTH AND MYSTERY

IS VOLUME

8

OF THE

Twentieth Century Encyclopedia of Catholicism

UNDER SECTION

I

KNOWLEDGE AND FAITH

IT IS ALSO THE

145TH

VOLUME IN ORDER OF PUBLICATION

Edited by HENRI DANIEL-ROPS of the Académie Française

MYTH AND MYSTERY

by *JEAN DANIELOU*

Translated by P. J. Hepburne-Scott

HAWTHORN BOOKS · PUBLISHERS · *New York*

First American Edition, June, 1968

NIHIL OBSTAT

Donald A. Panella, S.T.L., S.S.L.

    Censor Deputatus

IMPRIMATUR

Terence J. Cooke, D.D.

New York, N.Y., March 2, 1968

The nihil obstat and imprimatur are a declaration that a book or pamphlet is considered to be free from doctrinal or moral error. It is not implied that those who have granted the nihil obstat and imprimatur agree with the contents, opinions, or statements expressed.

9786

To the memory of Daniel-Rops

CONTENTS

INTRODUCTION

This book needs some explanation. It does not pretend to be a technical study on the ideas of myth and mystery. I use these words in their ordinary meaning. "Myth" here denotes all the representations through which men have tried to express their knowledge of God. "Mystery" denotes the revelation which God has made of himself in the Old and New Testaments.

The question this book tries to answer is one of language. How can we speak of God to the men of our day? Between the God who seeks man, and man who seeks God, the path must be found. Our speech about God must reach the heart of man, his inner experience. In particular, it must reach the heart of the man of our day.

This book is the expression of that attempt. It was first given in the form of lectures. I had to speak about God to an audience of young people. It is therefore in its very origin a dialogue, and has still the style of a dialogue. Before all else I had to lay the foundations of the essential affirmations, and it is above all on these foundations that the book insists. The manuals of theology are there for those who wish to go into more detail.

I had already tackled the subject in an earlier book, *Dieu et nous*. Some themes are therefore common to both. But I have been led to approach the questions afresh. Certain reactions, such as those of Francis Jeanson, have prompted me to emphasize fresh points. This is therefore a new stage in the exploration of the same subject. For more technical developments, I refer the reader to the earlier book. Here I have retained chiefly what concerned the fundamental proofs.

I realize the risks of such an enterprise. I should be the first to accept the criticisms of form and substance which may be made. I have chosen to incur these risks because, at a time when the existence of God is denied by so many minds, it is more than ever urgent that we should speak—and speak, I think, in that direct tone which may invite the criticism of the learned, but may more effectively reach men's hearts. And that is what matters.

CHAPTER I

THE MEANING OF
THE MYTHS

The first expression of man's encounter with God on the historical level is that of the ancient religions, before the revelation of God in the Old Testament. In this sense we can say that the fact of religion appears as a human fact, co-extensive with the history of man. Atheism is a modern fact, bound up with a certain set of historical circumstances, both sociological and psychological and with a certain set of conditions. From that point of view it is not in conformity with the fundamental needs of human nature. On any hypothesis it is certain that religion is one of the essential traits which mark the rise of the "human phenomenon," to use the language of Teilhard. Ethnologists insist that what enables us to recognize the presence of a man and not of an animal is, on the one hand, art, the tool, and on the other hand, worship, the rite. This human fact of a certain relation between man and God is realized historically at the level of the religions. Man's natural state is therefore paganism. Atheism is sub-natural, Christianity is supernatural; man is naturally pagan, that is, he has a certain reference to God. Now the grace of God does not destroy nature but expands it, so that paganism is recaptured, purified, and transfigured by the grace of Christ, but not destroyed. And in this respect we are always at a certain level of that transformation. This, by the way, makes me increasingly indulgent toward certain forms of Christianity which we are sometimes tempted to think superstitious or pagan, and which correspond to that barely transfigured residuum of paganism. Among intellectuals there is sometimes found a desire to purify Christianity completely of these elements, but this is very inhuman, and would make the faith such a rarefied atmosphere that most men could not breathe it. Christ is the act of God, who comes to seek man where he is and to raise him up to God. He comes to seek the poor, and by poor I mean the poor of all kinds, not only the poor in money. He comes to seek all the poor, the poor human beings involved in all the stress of human life, just where they are, and at first he is satisfied with very little, but that little is already something. If we tried to exclude from the Church all who are not "militants," we should end by reducing her to a little handful, shutting out all those who are not heroes, but yet have the right to form part of the Church.

By thus accepting the religious man, Christianity accepts the diversities of religious man. That is why the Word of God, which is the same for all—and that is the universalism of the faith—is variously received by an Indian, an African, or a Latin. Everyone, that is, receives this unique word of God under the form of his own religious makeup, and this is how the values of the religions are preserved in revelation. The diversities of the Church express, not the diversities of the faith, but the diversities in the manner of receiving the faith, so that an Indian who receives the faith remains perfectly Indian, and we, who are Greeks, Latins, or Gallic, remain perfectly what we are. Only we suffer from the illusion of thinking that our way of being Christians is the only way. We always have this illusion, and so we try to impose our way on others. It is the error, we may say, of missionary colonialism, and what is objectionable is not bringing Christianity but bringing it under its western form. In this respect the difficulties encountered by evangelization in various countries may have been legitimate. Where Christianity was destructive of the national religious values, the nations were in duty bound to refuse it, for it was attacking the integrity of the nation. But where the word of God is received according to the peculiar forms of the temperament of each people, it does not injure but rather reveals its values. Here again it is most important to distinguish revelation from religion. I said lately that it was absurd to change one's religion, but it is profoundly reasonable to change from religion to revelation, because this is an absolute advance, in which nothing of the former stage is lost, but all is taken up on to a higher plane. There must be neither rejection nor confusion, but all must be given its right place.

Christianity and paganism are not parallel but complementary. They represent two stages in the relation between God and man, the second being that of the biblical revelation, which is God's gift to man, God coming to meet man who seeks him. This relation is fundamental in our dealing with our pagan brothers, in order to show them that the gospel we proclaim to them demands no sort of denial of what they are, but simply represents its fulfillment. This is what enables Pope Paul VI to recognize the authenticity of Hinduism, not as a revelation of God but as a search for God, and thereby to inaugurate a valid dialogue. Here we touch fundamental categories, which enable us to form (as we shall in the first part of the book) a positive judgment on the value of the pagan religions, without in any way minimizing the transcendence of the Christian religion, and that is the important thing.

THE COSMIC MYTHS

Paganism is deployed on two levels: the meeting with God through the cosmos, and the meeting with God through man. Or, if you will, through nature and through consciousness. I need not say that in speaking of these things I am not venturing on archaeology, but everything I am saying is still valid today, with this difference (which at the end of this book will lead me to put some questions), that to the modern man the cosmos is apparently desacralized, in so far as man by his science has acquired a domination over it, so that it seems difficult to modern man to find God in nature. To ancient man there was nothing more sacramental, more "hierophanous," than the stars, because the stars were the expression of the inaccessible. The stellar world was a manifestation of the divine. Today the stellar world, at least at planetary level—in the sidereal world the goal is still far from achievement—is one of which man is gradually gaining control, and so it is being deprived in some way of its hierophanous value. In contrast (as I shall have occasion to say in concluding this chapter), the sphere of man is now an essential meeting-point between man and the sacred. The decisive human situations, such as love, death, freedom, are the points where an encounter with the transcendent becomes again remarkably possible. The contemporary pagan is not a pagan of the cosmos, but a pagan of man. He sees in human experience a certain element of transcendence and the sacred. But this "sacred" is perceived more clearly in the experience of love or of death than in the contemplation of the stars. This is an important point in the distinction between ancient and modern paganism. But both forms are genuine forms of paganism, and in fact, as I shall have to say, both forms already existed in ancient paganism.

The myths are, in the first place, the experience of a certain manifestation of God through the cosmos. The pagan man is the man to whom nature, the visible world, speaks of God, the man to whom the sun and its rays, the storm and the terror it arouses, the dew as a sign of blessing, convey a certain presence of God. The great masters of the phenomenology of religions, Eliade, Otto, and van der Leeuw, have shown that our image of the pagans is often a caricature, insofar as we imagine that they worship pieces of carved wood or the material stars. To the pagan, the material element is the sign, the symbol, and (to use the technical term dear to Eliade) the hierophany, that is, the manifestation of the sacred, of a transcendent and mysterious reality. Paganism, of course, easily degenerates into idolatry or magic: it takes for ends what are only means. But idolatry and magic, so far from being of the stuff of paganism, are the perversion of it. The great authentic pagans, whether of India or of Greece and Rome—here I need only name Plato, Plotinus, or Vergil—are not in the least idolaters or magicians. They are essentially religious men, who represent precisely the supreme points of greatness in the world of the great classical civilizations.

The pagan is one who recognizes the divine through its manifestation in the visible world. The great work of Mircea Eliade is a repertory of the chief hierophanies. The important thing is that in these different pagan religions, African, Australian, Chinese, or Greek, the same cosmological facts represent the same aspects of God. That is to say that, while these religions have had no influence on one another, they arrive at the same experiences and at a mythology which is similar in all of them. This shows that there is an objective value in symbols; the symbols objectively denote certain aspects of God, some his goodness, some his power, others his holiness. We are touching a domain which is on the borders of theology and poetry, for the great poet is also one who grasps the inner reality of material objects; to him the sun is not merely an atomic explosion but is also significant of mystery. That is why poetic knowledge always retains its value, even in the scientific world. There could be nothing more absurd than to think that science eliminates poetry, for science is always closed against certain dimensions of the real which poetry attains, and the intuition of the poet remains absolutely true, whatever the advances of the scientist. It is the height of absurdity to imagine that scientific knowledge exhausts the real. That is the error of "scientism." To claim that science exhausts all knowledge betrays a prodigious intellectual poverty.

This is true, not only on the level of revelation, but also on that of ordinary experience. (I am still speaking of the level of our common humanity, not yet of the Christian level, which I shall deal with later: I speak from the purely human level.) And what I venture to postulate here is a genuine, integral humanism, as opposed to the scientific, atheist humanisms of today, to which I absolutely deny the right to be genuine humanisms, insofar as they seem to me to testify to an impoverished human experience. I am not in the least contrasting the two experiences: it is not at all my belief that one must take up a position against science in order to exalt mysticism. But I do say that the complete man is one who is able to have a scientific approach to reality, and on the other hand to have a religious approach to the same reality. The same realities are susceptible of a scientific analysis and of a religious intuition; the absurdity would consist precisely in thinking that the scientific explanation resolved and absorbed the mystical intuition.

Here I touch fundamental problems, where it is essential to give a strictly reasoned justification of positions which are too often represented as affective protestations. This is not a case of defending some sort of sphere of sensibility against a certain positivism. On the contrary, it is a case of preserving an integral rationality, refusing to reduce man's rationality to its scientific and positivist aspect, but giving that religious knowledge its scientific dimension, by showing that it really corresponds to an aspect of the knowledge of being. This means that complete knowledge of reality implies also that religious dimension.

I said this à propos of the very remarkable fact that research into the history of religions has proved that the pagan religions, though none of them has influenced the others, converge, as it were, in their recognition that the same realities of the cosmos are symbols of the same metaphysical and spiritual experiences. A full list would be very interesting, but we cannot go into details. I can at least indicate some themes. There are the hierophanies of the celestial world, connected with the stars or the planets. One of the essential hierophanies in all religions is the sun. It appears as the manifestation of light, scattering the darkness, but also as that which makes all life possible by the warmth it emits. Here the sun is worshiped, not as a material object, but inasmuch as through it there is manifested a power both light-giving and life-giving. The sun is like a sacrament in the pagan world, being a visible sign of an invisible reality. There is a primitive sacramentalism which is precisely this pagan sacramentalism, in which material objects are already effective signs. They may not be effective signs of the grace of Christ, but they are effective signs of the manifestation of the love of God.

Neither the Old nor the New Testament rejects these signs, or rather, they condemn them only insofar as they become objects of idolatry. St. John, at the end of his Apocalypse, says that in the new Jerusalem "they need no light of lamp or sun, for the Lord God will be their light." We know that even in the Old Testament the Messiah is called *oriens ex alto,* like the sun rising over the horizon, the Sun of Justice. All these terms are in turn applied to the Christ, so that he appears as the new sun of the new creation, irradiating a life which is not merely cosmic but supernatural and divine. But from the sun of the cosmos to the sun of the new creation there is an ascending and gradual progress, and if the sun of the first creation is rejected by the Christian, it is not at all because it is considered to have lost its value, but because the brilliance of the new sun, which is Christ, is such that in a way it obscures the brilliance of the sun of the visible creation. A Christian is one who is so dazzled by the light of Christ that he no longer stops short at the cosmic symbols; not because these symbols have no value but because they are infinitely surpassed by the brilliance of a new sacrament. Here there is, as it were, a religious history, in which there is no renouncing, but in which, as St. Paul said about Moses, we advance from glory to glory. The creation already has its glory, but the new creation has a higher glory. And this is a true view of the pagan religions. We are no longer pagans, just because the sun of Christ is more dazzling to us than the sun of the first creation, but certainly not because the sun of the first creation has not still a great value!

This is particularly true of the universe as it is revealed to us by modern science. Its prodigious dimensions, both in time and in space, give us that vertigo, as Gregory of Nyssa calls it, in face of all that disconcerts and disorientates us, all that is absolutely unfamiliar, which constitutes a sign, a manifestation, of what historians of religions call the "wholly other," thus giving us a certain sentiment of the "immensity" of God. I often quote—too often, I know, but I like it so much that I don't hesitate to quote it—the beginning of Rilke's *Duino Elegies*. About the angels he says: ". . . and if one of them suddenly took me to his heart, I should fall down dead from the excessive power of his life, for the beautiful is nothing but the first degree of the terrible." To Rilke, the beautiful is sometimes so intense as to be unbearable, and that is very true. "That which can uncover the secret despair: a sun setting in a scarlet sky," as Péguy puts it. It means that there are some moments when certain spectacles of nature are almost unbearable. Further, we sometimes shrink away from things which cause us too violent emotion: we prefer easier emotions. There are certain works of art which sometimes make us afraid, and we would rather attend an operetta than listen to a Bach sonata, because it does not stir up such depths within us. We well know that if we agree to listen to the Bach sonata we agree to have degrees of depth stirred up. Now to Rilke the beautiful is only the first degree of the terrible. The beautiful, that is, is only the first analogy of the sacred, and so gives us an idea of what the unbearable intensity of God could be, if he came too near us.

So we can say that in a sense the poetical experience, in the fullest sense, is a first analogy of the mystical experience. I say the aesthetic experience in the fullest sense; that is, that in a certain experience of the beautiful there is something which mediates a first reflection of the experience of the sacred. And what I said of the aesthetic experience is still more true of the mystical experience. We are shy of the mystical experience precisely because it involves us in depths in which we do not at all want to be involved. We are afraid of God, as we are afraid of the beautiful, as we are often afraid of everything which, in fact, involves us in something too deep, because it is easier to live on the surface of ourselves than to agree to be involved in our depths.

What we must really try to find, through what I am saying here, is the experience of God as a concrete and existential reality. We are not on the plane of a rational demonstration, but on that of a presence of the living God through his manifestation in nature. It is not a matter of the emotions. It is really a matter of an intelligible grasp of a content of knowledge. It is absurd to confine the content of our knowledge to what is simply rationalist or scientific. In sensibility or imagination there is an infinitely precious grasp of the real, provided that we develop it into an intellectual grasp, and do not leave it on the level of evanescent affectivity, but extract from it its "noetic" content. This is true of all experience. We shall speak of love, of death, of human experiences, but this is also true of the experience of nature. And, to return to what I was saying just now, I am skeptical when I am told that nowadays the cosmos is desacralized. Really it is not so at all. To the normal man the cosmos is still absolutely sacred. One can, of course, dispose of the cosmos more easily by science. But the complete man is one who is still sensitive to the poetical and mythical experience of the cosmos, and is capable of grasping, through the cosmic realities, a certain knowledge of the invisible.

"Noetic" means that something real and objective is grasped by the intellect, and this is the important thing here. Men of our day very often consider that the only objective reality is the scientific and deny that poetry is objective. To them, everything that depends on poetic intuition depends on pure subjectivity, that is, on a domain in which one can say what one likes, merely projecting oneself. Going further, many of our contemporaries hold that religion is equally subjective, that it is entirely based on a personal need, not on an objective reality, valid for all. The mistake here is to think that science is the only grasp of the real, and that everything else is only a grasp of the self. Now, the affirmation of all those who believe in the intellect is that there are exercises of the intellect beyond the scientific intellect, and that they have an objective value as rigorous as that of the scientific intellect.

THE IMAGE OF GOD

' But God is manifested to pagan man not simply through the cycles of nature but also through the deeds of men. Man too is a hierophany, and the most marvelous of all. The Bible tells us in the first chapter of Genesis that man was made in the image of God, God's image in the world is man himself, man insofar as he is the masterpiece and summit of creation, which is the most perfect epiphany of God. In this sense—approaching the problem first on the level of the pagan religions—one of the essential aspects of the myths of the pagan religions is to show that all the human acts are first accomplished in a primordial world, that which Jung calls the world of the archetypes.

The great acts of love and the family, of work and hard labor, of war or peace, are supposed to have first existed in the world of the gods, before they existed in the world of men. The world of the gods is a sort of archetype, of which the world of men is a reproduction. I shall have to say in a moment how important this is for the problem of the rites, the rites being precisely a way of recharging, as it were, the acts of man from their divine archetypes. It is interesting to note that depth psychology has shown that the myths express the constant factors in depth psychology. This explains why we never tire of the ancient myths. The myths of Oedipus, of Alcestes, of Orestes or Antigone remain a continual source of inspiration, to Racine as to Cocteau. The situations recur, and ultimately are always the same. This explains the anthropomorphic nature of the myths. Reading Homer—the *Iliad* and the *Odyssey*—we are almost shocked to see the gods with the same morals as men. But this is something ontologically very profound about human nature.

This is important from the point of view of what I shall call the modern paganisms. I have said, and I maintain, that the cosmos is not desacralized: it is false to say that the world of today can no longer lead men to God, just because man has explored it. I maintain that it is a dimension of the visible world to be a hierophany, and that even when it has been explored from the scientific angle, it is still a hierophany from the poetic point of view. I still refer to the same categories. But all the same it is true—and here I must make some concessions—that it is more difficult to find God in a world where one knows all the works than in a world which is all the more a symbol of transcendence because it escapes our grasp. It is obvious that the starry sky seemed an outstanding symbol of transcendence precisely insofar as it was inaccessible, for transcendence is of its nature inaccessible.

And, of course, the inaccessibility of God is not the inaccessibility of the stars; that is simply a hierophany of the inaccessibility of God. But it is certain that for a child of today, who knows that men are soon going to the moon, the moon must seem largely desacralized, de-poeticized. So it is true that nature is less of a meeting point with the sacred for the modern man than it was for the man of former days, so that science has recaptured a number of things, not in the essential sense but nonetheless in a real sense.

I define my position very exactly, because these questions are much discussed at present. I maintain that we can still, today, go to God through nature, and that it is the really intelligent people who can do so. But it is certainly more difficult in proportion as nature is increasingly viewed as only a field of experience. But on the other hand there is certainly something else which the modern man finds increasingly a point of contact with the sacred, and that is man. The man of today has become sensitive to man. Everything which concerns man, man's dignity, the tragedy of the human condition, affects us today to an extraordinary degree. The nineteenth century witnessed an attempt to reduce man to nature, to see him as a simple example of the evolution of cosmic life. This still exists at the level of materialist evolutionism, and of a certain materialist Marxism. But it is certain that today those men who are charged with the destinies of mankind, those who have their hands on the controls of science, find themselves more and more aware that technology as such is powerless to resolve man's problems, and increasingly realize that man is something which cannot be reduced to mere matter. We can say that the learned of today are becoming more open to the mystery of man, which compels attention from the very fact of the development of science. This is, I think, one of the aspects of what makes the thought of Teilhard de Chardin, for example, so relevant, inasmuch as to him the human phenomenon appears to compel attention from the scientific point of view; that is, that the attempt to resolve man into nature, to make him only an accident of nature, seems to be impossible.

At this point there is an encounter between the modern scholar and man, a question addressed by the world of today to the religions and the philosophies, asking them: what is man? For if we don't know what man is, we may dispose of enormous resources, but we don't know what to do with them. We know too well that science can destroy as well as construct. Hence the fundamental problem: what is man? It was one of the essential questions raised at the recent Council, and answered in the Constitution on "The Church in the World of Today." Raising the problem of man means the encounter of science with a number of things which it considers irreducible. I shall take two of them. The first is the encounter of science with love. None of the demographical, biological or sexological points of view exhaust the personal mystery of the relationship of man and woman. For this does not concern solely the transmission of life. Love is not just an illusion which comes for a moment to a boy and a girl in order to propagate life, and then to cast them aside into the void. To the Christian, love surpasses the domain of the transmission of biological life. It is the relationship of two persons who absolutely transcend the world of life. The experience of a real love in this sense is something which cannot be doubted.

The other question is that of death. It is raised by the very progress of technology. On the one hand, it is possible to hasten death: the easy death of euthanasia. Man disappears without being conscious of it. The other possibility is the prolongation of a life which will not be able to rise again to the level of consciousness. Now the use of these techniques implies adopting a position toward death. It is certain that if death is only a descent into nothingness, then the more gently one descends into it, the better it will be. But if death is the beginning of eternal life, and if the confrontation with death is the chance for many men to perform the decisive acts of their life, it would seem wrong to deprive any man of that confrontation, for that would rob him of one of the essential occasions—perhaps the only essential occasion—of exercising his freedom. Most people pass existence by. A week's retreat enables one to exercise one's freedom and refuse to elude the decisive choices. But death at least obliges every man to make that choice.

It will surprise no one to observe that if today we want to find the myths of modern man, we should look for them in the best forms of the cinema. The films of a Bergman or a Buñuel are related to the myth, in the form of man's confrontation with the decisive situations. Modern man, often said to be the man of positivism, is in some respects the man of metaphysical anguish. But that metaphysical anguish is encountered essentially on the level of man and his destiny. It is in the decisive situations of his destiny that modern man encounters the sacred mystery, rather than through the cosmos. That is the great difference between the ancient and the modern pagan. The man to whom religion is essentially on the level of the myths of the contemporary cinema is not yet a Christian, not yet a Jew, but in some respects he is already a pagan. And for me to call someone a pagan is high praise! The pagan is open to disquiet about the absolute. He is not an atheist in the strict sense of a man who is finally settled in his self-sufficiency.

CHAPTER II

LITURGIES AND MYSTICISM

Having dealt with the myths, I turn to the two other essential aspects of the pagan religions: the rites and the forms of mysticism. These may be called the three constitutive elements of the religions. The myths are their intellectual, doctrinal aspect; the rites are their cultural aspect; the forms of mysticism are their inner experiences. What are the rites? If the myths are their way of affirming that man is in contact with God, the rites are their way of concretely making that contact. This is the object of the rites of all religions. The rites are the means of entering into communion with the divine, with the sacred, which is why they are an essential element of the religions. Further, they are always symbolic actions, but are regarded as channels of a mysterious efficacy. In this sense the rite has always an element of signifying and an element of effect. Christianity has come to define the sacraments as effective signs: a sacrament is an effective sign. From this point of view there is no difference, as to the general type, between the rites of the pagan religions, the rites of Judaism and the rites of the Christian religion. The rite is always both a sign and an effective power. I shall argue precisely that the content is different, that the efficacy of the pagan rites is not the same as that of the Christian rites, but not that they are other than parallel in form.

THE PAGAN RITES

To take some examples directly from rites found in all religions, the libation of water, the act of watering the ground, is an imitation of the rain, designed to produce rain. That is to say that when there has been a prolonged period of drought, men carry out rites of pouring out water, believing that these rites are charged with a certain efficacy, and that by performing this rite they will obtain rain. Here we are in a particular world, that of the mysterious correspondences between the different domains of reality. These rites need to be interpreted and pose an interesting problem. It is certainly one of the aspects of the pagan religions about which the modern scientific mind is most reticent, because it conceives everything exclusively in terms of efficient causality, and does not understand analogical causality, the fact that there may be a relation of causality dependent on a relation which is symbolic, not efficient.

In reality, if we ask ourselves whether the pagan rites are really efficacious, there are several possible explanations. The earliest Christians, who were very severe against the pagan religions, tended to interpret the pagan rites as being connected with magic, and to give them a demonic explanation. That is a possible explanation. The rite as such is not efficacious, but through the rite worship is offered to the demonic powers and it is these powers who operate. This raises problems about some practices which are still rather disquieting. It is certain that even the Church's position about them does not always succeed in being absolutely clear. Is it a communication with the devil? Is it something purely natural? The fact remains that this sort of thing has a great attraction for some rather elementary minds. In South America there has been an extraordinary development of spiritualism, and everyone knows that even today many Frenchmen and even more Frenchwomen pay attention to the horoscope. Many people think it very important to know whether they were born under the Ram or the Scorpion. This is one of the French shopgirl's forms of paganism. And in our world, which looks so positivist, religious aspirations which have been led astray will fasten on anything. But to have no religious aspirations is absolutely inhuman. I feel much nearer to the little shopgirl who consults her horoscope than to the intellectual who believes in nothing. She is mistaken in the way she applies her religious feelings, but her very mistake is a sign that there is, all the same, a mystery surrounding life, that everything is not reduced to a gross positivism. And this is again the expression, quite spontaneous and natural, of a certain religious spirit.

I said, then, that there can be a first type of explanation, the demonic. There is a second type, which would hold that there really is a causality proceeding from analogy, and that the act of imitating the rain produces the rain. This derives from a notion of analogical causality which is found in certain philosophies, whether those of antiquity (for example in astrology) or, equally, in certain African religions. But that interpretation, of a sort of causality simply analogical, seems scarcely defensible. One really cannot see on what it could be based. There is, however, a third explanation, which is not in the least magical, for the characteristic of magic is to try to constrain God, which is clean contrary to the true relation between God and man. But the pagan rite can be conceived thus: that the rite, which actually imitates the result one desires to see produced, expresses the conviction that the world is not ruled by blind determinism, but is governed by a living God. At this level the rite expresses the belief in God's intervention in the life of the cosmos and the life of man, the belief which is the basis of the pagan religions, and in itself is perfectly valid.

Does this mean that the rite is necessarily efficacious? Certainly not, and indeed experience shows clearly that it is not so. But this signifies—and this is essential—that there is a relation with God, not only on the subjective level but also on the objective level; that the cosmos depends on God, and therefore that it is legitimate to ask God to manifest himself, to manifest his providence through the cosmos. We know that this prayer, which consists in asking for God's intervention in the order of nature, is rarely granted. Yet it remains valid. I mean that the peasant's prayer for rain or fine weather, and the Church's liturgy, which has a special prayer for times of great drought, show that the Church rejects the concept of a universe without relation to God; she believes that through the order of the universe God intervenes and shows himself. To try to dissociate the cosmos totally from its dependence on God is to go against what is the very root of religious faith, the fact that as everything is created, everything depends radically on God. It is also true that God is very economical with his miracles, so that what I am saying does not mean that we believe, exactly, that God multiplies his miracles. But it means something very profound to the religious soul, and that is to know that we are in God's hands for everything, and that we must be able to trust everything to God, including his goodness in the natural order. It would be absurd if a child were not to pray for his parents' health. It would be positively inhuman. And when a child does that, he is absolutely right. This does not mean in the least that God will work a miracle, but it means that this idea, that in all things we are in the hands of God, is the very expression of the fundamental religious attitude. To want to dissociate the two planes, that is, to want to secularize completely all the natural side of our existence, and somehow to put our relation with God on the fringe of our real life, is precisely to deny the belief which is the foundation of religion, that we come to God and go to God through our whole selves; our relation with God covers and embraces every single thing in existence. There is nothing so serious in the modern world as the fact that there is this sort of dissociation between the domain of faith, which concerns the realm of religious practices, and a whole life situated on a plane which is not even pagan (since in my vocabulary to be a pagan is precisely to find God everywhere), but on the plane of a "laicism" or secularism which desacralizes absolutely everything and separates God from our daily life. In this sense the rite, insofar as it simply expresses the connection between God and daily life, is something in paganism which is entirely valid.

PAGAN RITES AND CHRISTIAN SACRAMENTS

What, then, is the present state of the question regarding the relation between the pagan rites and the Christian sacraments? At first sight we cannot help being struck by the extraordinary resemblance between the rites of all religions—a fact which often gives rise to a certain syncretism. In reality, the outward expressions of religion are the same everywhere. The rites are the same; the act of signifying communion with God by a meal, the act of signifying purification from sins by immersion in water, the act of signifying the communication of a mysterious power by an anointing with oil, are things which are common to all religions, because these rites are really expressions of a natural symbolism, and it is normal to start from this natural symbolism as a foundation for a religious symbolism.

Similarly, in all religions the sacred seasons and places are the same everywhere. The feasts are always kept at the same times, which are precisely the seasonal times. In all religions there are feasts at the beginning of spring, at what we call Easter; there are feasts at harvest time, at what we call Pentecost; there are feasts at the time of vintage—and from this point of view I am very sorry that the Jewish feast of Tabernacles, which was kept at this time, was dropped by the Church. There is the feast at the winter solstice, which is Christmas, and the most pagan of all the Christian feasts, for we all agree that no one knows when the child Jesus was born. There is no indication of it in the Gospels. This feast appeared in the fourth century, to take the place of the pagan feast which marked the point when the nights shorten and the days begin to lengthen, and so the feast of the birth of Jesus, who is the rising sun of the new creation, was fixed at that time. In the same way it has been shown that the feast of the Purification, with the rite of the candles, was an old pagan feast in connection with the Saturnalia. The Assumption is connected with the Phoenician feasts of Tammuz. It is the same with the sacred places. God has always been worshiped in the same places. Mont-Saint-Michel, long before it became a place of Christian worship, was an ancient holy place of the Celtic religions. Mount Carmel was originally the center of a cult offered to Astarte, the Phoenician goddess of vegetation. The prophet Elijah drove the priestesses of Astarte away and founded there a place of Jewish worship. And now, finally, there are pious nuns called Carmelites, who never suspect that they are the successors of the priestesses of Astarte, or that this title of their contemplative order signifies that Christianity wonderfully transcends the pagan religions, but does so by assuming them, and is not in the least ashamed to have a place, in some way, in that sequence.

There are some today who would like to purge Christianity of all these pagan survivals, and would throw the Christmas tree, the palms, and the Easter eggs into the fire. I would only say that if they ever do, the children will be in despair. Now, as Bernanos said, it is the children who are in the right, against the grown-ups, for this corresponds to nature. A child is not hungry for Christianity, but he is hungry for paganism. That is to say, a child hungers for a world in which there are not only positive things, but also the depths of mystery. Now the child is right in thinking that the world is marvelous, that it is filled with mysterious presences. That is how children are naturally little pagans. And so I say that even when a father is an atheist, it would be a crime for him to bring up his children without religion, for he would make them unhappy children. Education should consist in helping the child to progress from that pagan world to the Christian world, that is, to let him gradually understand that in Christ there is revealed something of God which surpasses what he first apprehended, but does not destroy it. It would therefore be a great loss to try, as some modern puritans would try, to eliminate from the Christian life all these Christianized pagan elements.

The important thing is that the signs, while remaining the same, are charged with a new meaning. Within the people of Israel the rites expressed the manifestation of Yahweh, no longer as Master of nature, but as the Lord of history. The Passover then no longer commemorated the seasonal renewal, but the going out from Egypt, the liberation of the people of God, and at the same time it re-enacted that liberation for the people. That is to say that at that moment the rite makes a historical event contemporary, in all the efficacy of that event. Thus we shall see that in Christianity the Mass makes present the sacrifice of the Cross. Already the Jewish Passover made present the going out from Egypt in its efficacy. This idea of a saving event (for here we are in history), but a saving event whose efficacy persists through its ritual imitation, radically differentiates the Jewish or Christian rite from the pagan rite, by relating it, not to the recurring cycles of natural life, but to God's intervention in history. Some excellent pages on this subject will be found in Robert Aron's book, *Les années obscures de Jésus*.

We find this again on a third plane, at the level of Christianity. What is then signified is the saving action of Christ. The same rite, of passing through the water—which at the level of the pagan religions signified simply the renewal of natural life, and at the Jewish level signified participation in the historic action of the Passover and integration into the people of Israel—now signifies, as St. Paul says in so many words, the imitation of the death and resurrection of Jesus, which works in us the effect of that death and resurrection. The man to be baptized went down into the water up to his shoulders. The priest asked him: "Do you believe in God the Father?" The man answered, "I believe," and the celebrant immersed him completely. This was repeated three times, in the name of the three persons of the Trinity. At this level baptism is the expression of a putting to death and a rising from death: the putting to death of the old man and the creation of the new man. It is a "configuration" to the death and resurrection of Christ, which brings about the effect of that death and resurrection. That is a sacrament. The sacramental causality is that of God, who works through the rite.

By means of the sacrament the man that he was, the "old man," is really destroyed. What is immersed, what is put to death, is the "old man," and what emerges is the new, risen man, who is clothed in the white garment, that white garment which expresses the glory of the baptized. St. Ambrose says in his *Catecheses* that this glory is so great that even the angels cannot bear it. The white garment symbolizes the shining radiance of the glory of the Spirit, who dwells in that man. And then the anointing with oil on the forehead, the royal anointing, signifies and effects the gift of the Spirit, communicating the graces of the kingship, the priesthood and prophecy.

But what is remarkable, precisely in the line of what I am trying to make clear, is that the same actions, the same seasons, and the same places which were first the expression of the cosmic religion, and then of the Jewish religion, have now become that of the Christian religion. Easter recapitulates the whole religious history of mankind and shows that Christianity is, in this sense, the culmination of all former history and not a religion alongside other religions. I say a recapitulation, if we realize three things: first, that Easter in the pagan religions is the anniversary of the creation of the world, which was created in the spring, and consequently it renews the world afresh from the sources of its creation; second, that Easter is, next, the memorial of Israel's deliverance, and consequently recapitulates the whole history of the ancient people; and third, that Easter is supremely the effective memorial of the death and resurrection of Jesus Christ, in which the religious history of mankind culminates and is fulfilled, and really effects that death and resurrection in us. We can now see how Christianity is genuinely not opposed to the former religious history, but rather assumes it in its entirety and gives it its goal and fulfillment.

All this brings us back again to the same fundamental themes, to which I return indefatigably, because that is what enables us to have criteria by which to consider the relations between religions. That is one of the things we most lack nowadays, when we are continually in confusion when it comes to defining the relation of Christianity to Judaism or the pagan religions. It is therefore indispensable to have fundamental criteria and to be able to articulate them, in order that they may become our principles of judgment, and so may help us in discussion with others.

MYSTICAL EXPERIENCE

The third aspect of the structure of the religions is mysticism. This raises the immensely exciting problem (one of the most interesting to me) of "comparative mysticism." Here again we obviously find an extraordinary resemblance at first sight between the testimonies of Hindu, Moslem, and Christian mystics. There are great mystics in all religions.

There have obviously been some men in India who have had an extraordinary experience of God. There are the great mystics of ancient Greece, like Plotinus, who tells us that he several times attained ecstasy, a union with God beyond all representations. There are very great mystics in Islam, particularly Al Allah (the subject of an admirable thesis by Louis Massignon), who wrote some mystical works of great beauty. There are great Jewish mystics, in the line of what is called the Cabala, or in works like the "Introduction to the duties of hearts." And if we compare these mystical texts with those of St. John of the Cross, what strikes us at first is certainly their resemblance. Here we find again a dimension of the religious man: the experiential dimension. Dogma is an intellectual expression, the rite is an active expression. Here we are in the order of experience, of man's interior grasp of God, as the climax of a whole effort of purification and concentration.

This experience of God takes various forms. It has a common form which may be called piety, that inner attitude of joy in God, of humble love of God, which we find in all religions, and in India is called *bhakti*. That personal religious experience, the experience of the soul with God, is found in all religions in the form of one of the fundamental structures of religious phenomenology: prayer. In fact prayer is something universal, the attitude by which the soul enters individually and personally into communication with the deity, whether under the form of adoration, when the soul is dazzled by God's transcendence, or under the form of gratitude, welling up to God from the depths of the soul at sight of the beauty of the world or of certain joys of existence. These are among the most fundamental sentiments of the human soul, prior to all revelation, revealing a fundamental authenticity which expresses something basically valid.

This is an aspect of the inheritance of integral human experience. Prayer is one of the great fields of the history of mankind, one of its privileged kingdoms. As there is a history of science and a history of art, so there is a history of prayer, from the sacred hymns of India to the prayers preserved by the religions of ancient Greece and the wonderful prayers bequeathed us by Persian and Arabian Islam. Here we always come back to a fact which is forced on us by a sort of overwhelming evidence: a world impoverished of that dimension might be far more advanced technically, but would be far less advanced on the level of inner experience, and in that sense it would be a far more inhuman world.

In these days we are so blinded by the technical aspects of humanism that we forget that it corresponds to only one of man's dimensions, and that prayer is another of his dimensions. This lies behind the protest that eastern countries like India have always made against a west which has so often betrayed its spiritual dimension, keeping only the scientific. In that sense, an Indian has every right to consider himself more civilized than a westerner, for if civilization means the full development of man at all levels of his existence, then a world in which no one prays, even if it is technically developed, is less civilized than a world in which men pray, though it is less advanced materially. We spoke of thanksgiving and adoration. There is also the humble prayer of petition, which is as old as human history, and is the spontaneous expression of man's awareness that he is helpless and limited, and of that absolutely true attitude (although its points of application may not all be equally valid) by which he looks to God for what can satisfy his heart. Its expressions are sometimes naïve; the prayers of a little child are for things we may think absurd. But that does not prevent this attitude from being genuine. It is the expression of that fundamental movement of exchange between God and man which is one of the dimensions of humanism.

Once again, what Christianity does for this existing human reality is to give it its full significance and fulfillment. In the pagan soul, that relation of the soul with God remains a groping, hesitant search. Christianity takes it over, leading it to its fulfillment. Christ is answered prayer. In him the infinite aspiration of all mankind for an intimate union with God is in fact satisfied by the total gift which God makes of himself. It takes two to be united. And if man seeks God, it is still necessary, if he is to be satisfied, that God should give himself. Otherwise we have only an infinite search, without object. Now Christ is precisely the gift which God makes of himself to man. That is why we can say that Christ is answered prayer, man's dream of union, fully come true. On the other hand, he is prayer attaining at the same time its supreme expression of complete intimacy with the sphere of the divinity, by the very fact that through Christ, as the Epistle to the Hebrews says, we have access to the Father, and that only in the Spirit can we say: "Abba; Father." In other words, the striving of prayer to be an intimacy with a God who is Father and Loving, foreshadowed in the pagan religions, actually becomes, through Christ, a sovereign reality, so that we are called children of God, "and so we are."

This interior experience is expressed in its highest forms in what we call mysticism. I mean that the spiritual experience—prayer—is as extensive as all mankind. Sinners and saints, old men and children, all alike pray. Prayer, we may say, is coextensive with the integral human experience. But mysticism is something more. It is man's attempt to arrive at a more perfect union with God, to be fused into him. Here, in the religions, we are faced with a very important domain which concerns all the forms of asceticism and the techniques of the inner life, by which men in all religions have tried to get beyond the realm of superficial life, to be "interiorized," to be recollected, to attain a degree of silence and inner detachment, in order thus to become more capable of a union with God. Again, this is nothing specifically

Christian, and I would even say that in the last resort it need not be specifically religious.

For Hinayana Buddhism, for example, mysticism means detaching the real self, our deepest, innermost core of existence, but not in order to enter into communion with a personal God. But the essential thing is always the effort to detach oneself from the disturbance of the external world and, more profoundly, to detach the will from the many and varied desires, so as to unify the soul beyond all particular things. This mysticism, then, is quite general in character. Its forms are all in fact the same. It is a striking fact that, whether one takes Hindu Yoga, Japanese Zen, neoplatonic catharsis, or elementary manuals of prayer—"the practice of mental prayer for the use of beginners"—one always finds the same method.

But the trouble is that one does not recollect oneself just for the sake of being recollected; one does so for some object. And it is over the question of the object of that recollection that the divergence between the various mysticisms begins. This technique can in fact be simply a certain way of discovering oneself, one's inner being, one's real self. Roughly speaking, that is what is represented by the Stoic wisdom, which was primarily a certain way of becoming invulnerable to events. The basis of Buddhism is in a sense very simple: man's problem is to escape suffering; suffering comes from desire; the only way to avoid suffering is to desire nothing; the man who is truly detached from everything does not suffer from anything, since he no longer wants anything. This may be a disappointing philosophy, but it certainly is a philosophy.

On a much deeper level, in the pagan religions as a whole, mysticism is found as a way of union with the deity. If the soul enters into itself, it discovers, through itself and in a way beyond itself, the mysterious source from which it emanates. And in this sense we can say that the inner experience is connected with the definition I gave of all the religions, which is a search for God. But here the search for God is not through contemplation of the outer world but through rediscovery of the inner world, that is, one discovers God through oneself. And this is perfectly true, that our inner being, our person, is something which comes from God, which flows from him all the time and, as the Bible itself says, is in a way his image. It is then a rediscovery of God through oneself, by the discovery of that mysterious source from which our life perpetually flows.

Through this inner experience a certain grasp of God is obtained, and this grasp of God is essentially linked with the fact that between the soul and God there is a fundamental relation, so that by this return to itself the soul can discover a certain presence of that God from which it flows all the time as from its source. For "to exist" means to receive oneself at every moment from God. At the depth of ourselves, beyond ourselves, there springs up perpetually that gift of ourselves which God makes to ourselves. And we can well understand that in this return to oneself, when one has passed the successive stages of sensation and visible things, of the understanding and reasoning, when one has attained a certain inner silence and concentration, the soul, thus finding itself, and precisely beyond itself, emerges into something which is that "beyond the self" described for us by the great mystics. And this corresponds to a perfectly valid experience.

PAGAN MYSTICISM
AND CHRISTIAN MYSTICISM

The experience of the Christian mystics is certainly not of the same kind. The psychological processes are very similar, just as the ritual acts were almost the same, and the symbols were almost the same. But again we are faced with the essential difference between the natural religions and the Jewish-

Christian revelation: the experience of natural mysticism is simply that of a search for God. By an effort of concentration the soul succeeds in going, in a way, beyond itself and arriving at what Philo called a search without form, but it is still of the nature of a search. The very definition of a revelation is that it is the inverse movement, that is, a coming of God to us, and what the Christian mystic finds is the presence in himself of something which is given him and does not come from himself at all. The essential characteristic, from the point of view of the difference, is that natural mysticism depends on a technique of inwardness, so that it is by his own effort that man finally reaches the goal, whereas the Christian mystical experience is essentially that of a gift to which we must open ourselves but which utterly surpasses all that man could ever come to grasp by his own powers.

The characteristic of the Christian fact is that God gives himself. At this level, the mystical experience is no longer a mere groping search for a fundamental unity in which one aspires to be dissolved. It is essentially a meeting with a "thou," a living person, with whom one enters on a dialogue of love, and who therefore appears as revealing himself in his otherness. The Christian mystic feels that he is being invaded by a strange presence which sweeps him off his feet, and with which he feels drawn to enter a communion of love. We have here an example of the manner in which the gift of God in Christ comes to capture, as it were, the natural religious experience, in order to lead it to its climax. In the words of Fr. de Lubac, we must not separate mysticism from mystery. Mysticism without the mystery, that is, the religious experience which does not meet with Christ, is something which remains uncertain. It is what we often feel, for example, about the eastern mystics. But on the other hand, the mystery without mysticism, that is, the Christian faith when it does not become prayer and inwardness, is in danger of becoming formalism. This is the case with all Christians who have no interior life. They have the mystery, insofar as they believe, but they have not mysticism, insofar as their faith is not inwardness.

That is why the comparison between the absence of mystics in the west and their presence in the east often leads certain westerners to wonder whether the truth may not have deserted the west, to be found in the east. This is that return to the east, which we have met in some of our contemporaries; it is what causes the ashrams of India to be partly populated by American widows, and in general by westerners in search of a liberating inwardness. But this is to look at things from the point of view only of the intensity of the religious experience, not of the truth of the faith. In the end, the mystery is more important than the mysticism. I mean that in the end it is faith, as Paul says, which is the essential thing, for in the end it is Jesus Christ who saves. One is not saved by the inner experience. Salvation is not something we give ourselves. The problem is not to find the best *bhiksu,* the best instructor in the methods of the inner life, for after all the *bhiksu* himself needs to be saved. As St. Paul says: all have sinned and need the grace of God: the most "interiorized" sage as much as the most "exteriorized," ordinary sinner, because it is grace that saves, not the interior life. But this saving grace comes to take hold of those values which are the values of man, and it bears fruit all the more in a soil which is religiously developed. And that is why the saints, those whom we call the saints, are precisely those in whom saving grace has borne fruit, because it has met with a very great wealth of inner life. But as for those who have none of that inner life, grace lights on them indeed, but in a way which remains external, not penetrating them from within. They will have travail in purgatory. Grace must refashion and repossess us completely. So prayer is a sort of advance drawn on purgatory.

This is very important, because one of the great mistakes

of our day is to think that it is mysticism that matters. It is the attitude of those who say: it doesn't matter what dogma you believe, the important thing is to be men of interior life. Now, we say just the opposite. The essential thing is that Jesus Christ has brought us salvation, and in reality that is the only thing that saves. To be men of interior life, well, we must try to be so as much as possible: we do what we can. But it is the glory of the Christian affirmation that in it salvation is also offered to the poor. Salvation is not simply the privilege of a little élite of ascetics, sheltering in their sacred mountains, but of all who have come to believe in Jesus Christ. So the important thing is that fundamental attitude of humility which makes us open ourselves to the faith of Christ. For the rest, I repeat, each man does what he can. It is not always in our power to devote enough time to prayer for the mystery to lead us on to mysticism.

The mercy of Jesus Christ is this, that salvation is not reserved for mystics, and that is a wonderful thing. For the Buddhists or the neoplatonists, salvation is reserved for the mystics, the saved are the mystics. For us it is not so. The saved are those who have put their trust in God's act of love in Christ, mystics or no. But again, we must try to be mystics, each at his own level. Not necessarily mystics who have ecstasies. But the need to make our faith inward is in fact a grave duty. That is how it becomes really personal. But things must be put in their right places, the different domains must not be confused: that is what I am trying to do. We must fix the levels where they belong. And the problem we have just approached is one of those we meet most often. At first sight the objection seems striking: there are holy men in Hinduism, there are holy men in Christianity. Why be a Christian, if the important thing is to be a holy man? That is what we have to be able to answer, and the answer is precisely what I have said, that salvation is that free act which is given in Jesus Christ, not something resulting from the perfection of a technique of interiorization. If it were, we should be in precisely the position we have all rejected, with St. Paul, St. Augustine, Luther, Pascal (for here Catholics, Orthodox, and Protestants are all agreed), namely, that salvation is the work of man and not of Christ. The very ground and starting point of it all is St. Paul's assertion in the Epistle to the Romans: "All have sinned and fall short of the glory of God." That is to say that as regards salvation all are on the same footing. A man is not saved first for his merits, he is saved because of his faith. The essential thing is that the truth which is in fact essential—that Jesus Christ has come into the world to save us from the misery from which we cannot escape by ourselves—should be believed by us.

That is why religion does not save. Religion, as I have said, is the search for God. But the gulf dividing man from God, which man cannot bridge, God alone has bridged, and Christ is the bridge. The essential is that this has been done, and it is done from now on. The gulf has been bridged. In Christ we have access to God. We believe it, and thereby we are saved. Many men have not been able to believe it, either because they lived before Christ, or today, because they do not know it. These too can be saved, but they too will be saved by the saving action of Christ. Millions of Hindus will be saved, but not because they have practiced yoga. That is the essential question: that is the idea which must be decisively eliminated. It is not yoga which saves, it is Jesus Christ, and so the Hindus who will be saved will be saved because the Word of God has come into the world, and because in his infinite love he will gather both all who have known him and believed in him, and all who did not know him, but yet were men of good will. They too will be gathered in by Jesus Christ, and then they will discover, in the light of the heavenly vision, the meaning of that action of Jesus Christ which they did not know on earth.

CHAPTER III

THE WEAKNESS OF
THE MYTHS

Religion is the realm of the search for God, a search which, as I have said, is part and parcel of the depth of the human soul. But to seek God does not mean to find him. Further, will the God whom we may find through seeking be the true God? I mean, will this God who will be within our reach at the end, be the true God? That is precisely the question we must ask.

I have repeatedly said that the religions have something which is valid. They are the expression of the religious man, and to my mind man is religious by nature. This is what is expressed in all forms of paganism, whether historical, in the past, or future, in all the forms of the search for God in the world of tomorrow. But on the other hand this search is a search in the dark; it is man, faced with the mystery which he seeks, who tries to express it and grasp it. But he cannot do it: it is what St. Paul refers to when he speaks of the nations "feeling after him." As Emil Brunner, the Swiss Protestant theologian, has said, "there is no religion without its profound truth: there is no religion without its profound error." And in fact when we examine either Hinduism or the African religions, we are constantly surprised to find, all the time, amazing religious intuitions and, a moment later, weird and distorted things which stagger and shock us. There is always something of a mixture, because this is the work of the human genius. It is clear that when we turn to the Jewish or Christian revelation the problem will be quite different, because here we are no longer looking at the creations of the genius of man, like the religions. The religions are the greatest of the creations of the genius of man, greater than the creations of science. But they are still only creations of the genius of man. They do not present us with something which has the actual authority of God.

It is important, therefore, when studying the religions, to distinguish what is valuable from what is not, for they always reveal deviations. These deviations can in general be grouped under three main heads, corresponding in practice to the three great groups of pagan religions. The first is polytheism, which is the popular form of deviation. To the pagan man, everything is full of divine presences, the oaks and the springs, the rocks and the thunder, the starry sky and the silence of the forest. And, as I said, it is human to be sensitive to this. But the descent is easy from a presence of God in the theophanies to a divinization of the things of the cosmos themselves. It is the ancestry of polytheism given by St. Paul in the beginning of his epistle to the Romans, to the effect that from the beginning of the world men were able to know God through his creation, but they have turned away from the true God to worship serpents, birds, and reptiles. Here he was alluding to actual facts; in Canaan men worshiped serpents, in Egypt they worshiped the sacred bird.

There is confusion, then, between created things and the Creator God, and that is called idolatry, which consists in treating the created object as divine. It is a confusion between the domains of the created and the uncreated. It is the great popular deviation. This is why Christian authors and the Bible are so severe against paganism. To them paganism means polytheism, because paganism is always more or less mixed with polytheism. In a Christian society we can be more tolerant, for we are less tempted to polytheism. In one sense, we should almost be tempted in the opposite direction, to lose sight of what is still valid in paganism—I mean the sacredness of the cosmos. There has to be a very delicate balance. But again, the danger for us is not to worship too much, the danger is rather not to worship at all. The polytheist is one who worships too much, who sees the divine even where it is not. In a sense, the polytheist temptation is easily explained. The world of polytheism, that world peopled with sacred presences, has something very alluring about it. It is a world peopled with divine presences. There is here a kind of experience. That distant murmur of the gods which the pagan heard in the forest or in the sea is something we could almost feel. The place of the gods has been taken by the angels, to express in some way that spiritual density of the cosmos, at the level, however, *not* of subordinate deities, which is an absurdity, but of creatures, representing a world of intermediaries.

PANTHEISM

The second deviation is much more important and more fundamental: it is pantheism. This is the metaphysical temptation. As polytheism is the popular temptation, so pantheism is the intellectual temptation. And it is on this rock that the higher religions—Hinduism, stoicism—have foundered.

This temptation can easily be explained. It falls in with a certain inclination of the human mind toward an ultimate reduction to unity. The basis of pantheism is the idea of a fundamental unity of all things, a unity in which the frontiers between God and man disappear. Creation is seen as an emanation from the divine substance, tending to be reabsorbed into itself, following a movement of expansion and then of re-collection. The creation is nothing else but God. But God exists in two states, a concentrated state and a diluted state. But it is the same thing—everything is the same. The consequence is clearly very important. We are God by nature; our being is divine. We become again this God that we are, when we move from the external and the multiple to the internal and the one. At bottom, to recover one's own unity is finally to coincide with the absolute unity, in which we are ultimately reabsorbed.

For this reason, pantheistic mysticisms are always mysticisms of the ultimate reabsorption into the one. To keep one's individuality is to remain still in imperfection. The true God is impersonal, and it is precisely by surpassing the limits of the personal life that one ends by rejoining the fundamental, radical unity. This is the very foundation of Indian mysticism. The *atman,* the individual soul, is a manifestation of the *brahman,* the absolute soul, and the *atman* is destined to be dissolved in the *brahman.*

Here we come to the radical originality of the Christian God, on the two essential points, the Trinity and Creation. What we have described is opposed by these two fundamental affirmations. The Bible, in fact, sees the creature as radically distinct from God. This is what is called transcendence; there is an abyss between the two. The creature has its source in God, not at all as a sort of diffusion of God, but because God has set it in his presence by a free act. It is radically other, and can in no manner be equal with God, who is totally beyond its reach. What makes the fundamental difference between all the pantheistic doctrines and the Jewish-Christian religion is the idea of transcendence, of the inaccessibility of God, and of the fact that we can only possess God if God freely gives himself to us, but we can never in any way be his equals, because we are simply of another nature.

This perspective brings to light another aspect. It is that union with God is essentially a meeting of love between two persons. God is a personal God who places a personal man in his presence. Consequently the union lies in the reciprocal gift. Therefore, if the love is to last forever, the difference between them must last forever. This means that the disappearance of the difference by fusion in the unity is something that destroys love, for it takes two to love. Here we find the ultimate foundation of the Christian mystery. It is not only that it concerns a personal relation between God and his creation, but that God is eternally not only two but three. That is to say that love is coextensive with being. Therefore —and this is a radical metaphysical difference—the basis of being is not a unity in which all will finally be resolved; the contrast is not between the one and the multiple, but the three is part of the structure of the absolute. The three is coeval with the one. The absolute is both at once, three and one. Which means that the absolute is love. This is the very foundation of the Christian revelation, and for metaphysics it is a paradoxical absolute. For all systems of metaphysics give the primacy to unity, and treat multiplicity as an imperfection. The paradox of the Christian revelation is that the Trinity is constitutive of the absolute. But this is something that no human intellect by itself could ever have discovered. If love and the Trinity are constitutive of the absolute, then the value of the human person and the idea that its relation to God is an interpersonal relation of love and not a dissolution in unity, follow as a natural consequence. So here we have two radically different types of thought. This, again, does not detract from what was valid in this nostalgia for unity, but it reveals another dimension of being, enabling us to penetrate further into the abysses of the mystery. And this is what Revelation is, going beyond the search which marked the pagan religions and letting us touch the manifestation of the very ground of being. It is the abyss itself, inaccessible to our grasp, which thus reveals, unveils, manifests itself to us.

Creation does not proceed from a necessary diffusion of God, but from a totally free act, and on the other hand the existence given to it has consistence, so that we have before us a personal, free God and the human person. On this level the relation to God appears in a totally different light. It does not tend toward a sort of final reabsorption in the one or the absolute, but toward a dialogue of eternal love, for which God brings us into existence, by giving us a consistence of our own, to make of us the God to whom he will communicate his gifts.

Beyond this dialogue of God and man and beyond this metaphysics of love, the Christian revelation, by introducing us to the depths of that being which is inaccessible to our reason, admits us to that mysterious truth that the absolute is itself tri-personal; that is, love is coeval with being. This is the last word of the Christian metaphysics. Being is love, because being eternally consists of an exchange of love. This is utterly beyond the reach of what human reason, left to itself, can attain. This is precisely the abyss into which the revelation of Christ introduces us, in which the Persons, who are that abyss, come to us, so as themselves to lead us into that very foundation of being, which is what they are themselves. And that, finally, is the whole Christian mystery, namely, essentially trinitarian life: both a discovery of the mysterious Trinity and a call to share in that life of the Trinity, by becoming, in the only Son, sons of the Father and temples of the Spirit.

We can therefore say that all Christianity is summed up in the revelation of the Trinity. Still we must understand how deeply and radically significant this is and how profoundly it concerns our life and solves its fundamental problems. For in the end all love—and it is essentially love which gives us the key to all our problems—is based on the fact that being is substantially love. At the end of his priestly prayer, in the passage which is his last will and testament, Christ said: "That they may be one, even as we are one, I in thee and thou in me." That is, he gave, as model for the unity of Christians in the ecclesial community, the unity of the Trinity in that trinitarian community. He showed us that what we are called to is a real sharing in that which constitutes the very ground of our existence. This brings it home to us that Christianity is not something superadded to reality, but the view which penetrates the abysses of reality; in other words, it is the profoundest view. This does not mean that there is no reality in more superficial views, but that here we are introduced to reality's deepest abysses.

DUALISM

There is still a final deviation demanding our attention: it is dualism, the theory that there are two principles, a principle of good and a principle of evil. Here too, as always, this deviation has appearances of truth. There is no denying that in the world as we see it there really are forces of good and forces of evil, and that we ourselves feel deeply torn between these opposing forces. Dualism tries to explain this obvious fact. In its extreme forms it postulates two principles on the same plane, whether of two divinities, as in the ancient Persian religion, or of opposition between the One and matter, as in Platonism. But in fact the most common form is a subordinated dualism, which itself has various degrees, some of which are true. We thoroughly believe in the existence of the powers of evil. In that sense, Christianity implies a certain dualism, not at the level of the constitutive principles of being (for the sole absolute principle is the good), but at the level of a degradation, a deformation, of the created being. Consequently the dualism exists, not at the level of God, but within creation. The evil powers are good powers which have been perverted.

The problem here is, at what level does this perversion exist? Here we meet one of the most important forms of dualism: gnosticism, which later became Manichaeism. From some points of view its idea is attractive. The gnostics start from the fact that the world is badly made. That is something evident, as it were. The world gives the impression of the absurd and the arbitrary. It is often the good who are unfortunate, the bad who succeed; and why are children born diseased? From this the gnostics conclude that the world cannot have been made by a good and intelligent God; it was made by a sort of inferior demiurge. The world itself, such as it is, is part of these degraded realities. The gnostics draw this conclusion, that the world being badly made, we must free ourselves from it, and that what is revealed by Christ is a radical condemnation of this world.

The Christian viewpoint is different. It holds that this world is good and is the work of God, that this creation, which surrounds us and which we are, has been made by a God who is wise and good. But this creation has been perverted at various levels, which are the levels of the mystery of evil. They are the liberties which have spoiled the working of this universe. These liberties are not in the first place human liberties, but those of mysterious powers beyond our control. Hence the importance in Christianity of the mystery of evil. Mankind is under the dominion of a power of perversion. It is the center of a spiritual drama, in which man is the stake, but which is first played out beyond the powers of man. Therefore, as I have already said, man cannot by himself arrange everything. Otherwise we should be in the realm of morality. Otherwise Jesus Christ would only have had to give us good examples and good advice. Now, in practice morality settles nothing, and the teachers of morality only succeed in making us more unhappy, for they tell us what we must do, but do not give us the ability to do it. We know too well that we need more than good advice; we are glutted with good advice. What we need is to be saved. We know in the depths of our hearts that salvation is not a matter of good will, that there are fatalities which imprison us. And it is precisely these fatalities, this mystery of evil, that the Word of God himself, coming into the world, has faced and destroyed. That is why the Son of God came into the world, not to give us good advice but to die and rise again. Jesus is not one teacher of morality among other teachers of morality. He is not a sort of Socrates, even a superior Socrates, for Socrates saved no one. Jesus Christ is the Saviour, he who has really faced the forces of evil and misery in their very roots, who has descended into hell, into the very depths of misery, and having reached those depths of misery, has destroyed those powers of evil and thus made us free, insofar as we believe in him, so that we are no longer under their power. Anyone who does not precisely understand this dramatic dimension of Christianity and reduces Christianity to morality, empties it of all its meaning. For after all, if it is good advice we want, Buddha gave excellent advice. People say that Christianity is summed up in love of our neighbor. But men did not have to wait for Christianity to love their neighbors. There is love of one's neighbor among the Buddhists, in all religions, among the communists.

Consequently this is not what constitutes Christianity. What does constitute Christianity is to confess that we do not love our neighbors, and because we don't love our neighbors we know that we need to be set free from those powers which prevent us loving our neighbors, which prevent the spiritual energies and the energies of love which are in us from being able to develop. And this is precisely the need which is specifically met by the salvation, the redemption, given by Christ: our need to be saved from evil, because we know very well from our experience that by ourselves we are unable to conquer the evil, to conquer it in ourselves and to conquer it in others.

Polytheism starts from something very true, that the springs, the fountains and the oaks are filled with sacred substance, but it interprets this wrongly. Pantheism starts from a true observation, that there is a profound unity between God and his creation, but it wrongly interprets the relation between God and the world. Dualism starts from a true observation, that we live in the midst of a conflict of good and evil, but it interprets that true observation wrongly. The religions never possess the truth completely, even on the metaphysical level. So it is, in fact, in the revelation of Christ that certain even natural truths find their complete development. This was what Pius XII pointed out in his encyclical *Evangelii praecones,* when he said that Revelation does not destroy the values of the religions, but purifies, assumes, and transfigures them. These attempts of man through the ages to draw men to God—and this is constitutive of man, as I said, and admirable—are still mixed with falsehood, and never quite reach their goal. That is why Christ, coming to win back men, also wins back the religions, to lead them to realize fully the virtualities which are in them. For a pagan, therefore, that is, for one who is on the level of the natural religions, to be converted does not mean to deny or to betray anything; it means to integrate, in a more perfect perspective, the authentic values contained in his religion.

CHAPTER IV

REASON AND THE EXISTENCE OF GOD

Man's personal encounter with God is the essence of religion. But unless we can provide a rational foundation for this encounter we lay ourselves open to the criticism of the rationalists, who hold that religion is the relic of a pre-logical view, that is, that it has consisted in giving supernatural explanations of things for which men did not yet know the natural explanation. This is the slogan we often find in more or less rationalist handbooks. When the laws of meteorology were unknown, men imagined that snowfall or sunshine were due to the will of higher powers; now that we know the scientific laws we eliminate that supernatural element. On these lines, science would gain step by step over religion, so as finally to eliminate it altogether.

It is therefore important to show that to be religious does not mean simply to respond to a certain inner experience, but also to be logical and not merely pre-logical. It is essential to show that while the encounter with God is in the first place existential, it is in the second place perfectly demonstrable by the strictest intellectual standards. In this respect we must not let ourselves be in the least impressed by those who claim that from the point of view of the intellect it is impossible to produce rational foundations for belief in the existence of God.

It is important to mention this, for in fact many Christians today are convinced that God can only be known by faith, and that on the intellectual level it is impossible to provide serious justification for belief in God. This is an abdication on the part of the intellect. So it is important to defend the intellect and to show that this little creature is not useless, but can serve, not only to discover the laws of the cosmos—as of course it does brilliantly today in scientific progress—but also to give access to another order, not of the laws of matter but of what lies beyond physics. The intellect has access to this; it is capable of knowing the realities of an intelligible order, and knowing them with a certitude which completely justifies the right of a fully lucid, perfectly critical man to hold that belief in God is not simply the result of an impulse of the heart, but stands up perfectly to all the criticisms of reason.

The question of the proofs of God's existence must therefore be broached. The difficulty is not that there are not enough of them, but that there are too many. This multiplicity of proofs might mean either of two things. It could mean that, if there is still discussion as to what the proof is, it is because it has not yet been found, just as we might say that we have not yet discovered the way to make interstellar journeys: it has not been reached; no doubt men will advance further. In this case, the multiplicity of proofs would simply mean that the real proof has not yet been found.

But it could equally well mean something else. I mean (and I would emphasize this point) that from the first philosophers who have pondered the question down to our contemporaries, the argument has in practice always been the same, and it is fundamentally valid. It always starts from the given fact of existence and shows that this fact does not contain its own explanation of itself. But the diversity of proofs is simply a diversity of starting points. These in fact differ according to differences of period, context, or temperament.

FROM TRUTH TO THE TRUTH

The starting point may be the actual exercise of the intellect, the intellect reflecting on its exercise. The starting point is the inner world. This was the argument followed by St. Augustine, who reflected on this inner life of man. What strikes him when he turns in on himself, and especially when, in so doing, he questions himself about what he does or does not believe, what then forces itself on him is the inescapable fact that it does not depend on him to believe one thing and not another; in other words, it is not he who establishes the truth or falsehood of things. They force themselves absolutely on his mind, not, of course, in the form of their palpable existence, but in the form of the basic justification which enables him to form a judgment of existence, saying: "This is true, that is false."

Now, Augustine asks, if it is not I who decide this, if the foundation of truth and morality is not my intellect, if I feel sure that I have not the right to organize things according to my own desire, but am obliged to submit to a reality which forces itself on me, the reason must be that there is in me, acting somehow in me, something which is greater than me; in other words, that it is not I who make the good and the true, but that the good and the true are things that I recognize as existing beyond and outside me. It is this submission to reality which constitutes, to Augustine, the primary experience from which he starts to reflect. He finds, in other words, that his personal experience is not the final goal to which he attains, but that it opens his eyes to a reality which surpasses him, or rather, in the very modern term he uses, is in himself more interior than himself. This is his famous saying: "One who in me is more myself than I." One, that is, in whom I recognize myself more than in myself, for in fact my own self is an evanescent self, a self which often escapes me, and I recognize what I know to be the truth in a reality which surpasses myself, and which I find, when I enter into myself, to be in myself, beyond that which is the real root of my being. This is the point St. Augustine developed, showing that every intellect is enlightened by the Word, of whom St. John's Gospel says that he enlightens every man coming into the world. Then from that point, developing and expanding certain great intuitions of ancient philosophy, he shows me in my own logos, that is, in my intellect in the fullest sense, a participation in the Logos as such, in him who is intellect and speech in himself, and in whom every intellect is a participation; he who is in some way the source of the light which, enlightening my intellect, enables it to reach the truth.

Why do so many men today refuse to accept this proof? It is not primarily because they do not believe in God, but because first they do not believe in truth. It is obvious that what we are now up against is not, first, a doubt of God but a doubt of man. By this I mean that we cannot advance from a certain experience of truth to the existence of an un-created truth unless we first hold that there is such a thing as truth. Similarly, if a man considers that there is no good or evil, that it is I who decide what is good or evil, and that putting myself in the place of God I consider myself the prime source of everything, that man cannot possibly start from the created reality to mount up to the uncreated reality, because in the first place this is to deny the existence of a *created* reality, it is to make everything originate from the claim of the human mind to constitute itself and to suffice to itself. Now it is precisely this which, not from the religious point of view, but on the plane of the simply human per-spective, seems to me to be absolutely untenable. The defect here is not an inability of the mind to mount to God, but the possibility of the mind being radically depraved. From the starting point of this depravation it is impossible to arrive anywhere, but here it is on the level of man that the challenge exists. And now we come to the essential problems of today. It is evident that if we are in a world which does not believe in the existence of a truth, if we are in a wholly subjectivist world, in which, as Pirandello says, every man has his own truth, if the men of our time believe that one can think anything, say anything, do anything, then it is impossible to bring out of nothingness anything else but nothingness. But then one is in a state of nothingness, and in a state of sheer hypocrisy, for in fact those who say this cannot translate it effectively into reality. For this would mean, as Claudel has so well said, that nothing has any importance, and that is sheer nothingness. But in fact many of those who advance this view in theory do behave after all in a way which gives the lie to their explicit statements.

Sartre lays down his theses, but in his personal relations he behaves with a generosity of heart which proves that he recognizes certain values. He violently takes sides in certain struggles, in the capacity of that moralist which he is in every fiber of his being, like every good Frenchman in the first place, and like every good French university man in particular, which means that he is steeped in morality. And in practice this really restores a morality, while he denies by his principles that any morality exists. Or a man like Malraux, in quite a different line, whose principles profess that the only ethic is that of personal experiment, is yet able to rise above his personal problems and to hold that there are things like the service of one's country which objectively deserve to be accepted. In the last resort, both end by restoring in action the objective statements which they deny in theory.

But then arises this problem: insofar as I am moved by such and such values and not others, why do these values impel me, why is there a truth or a goodness which absolutely compel my respect? If we reflect on this we see that this goodness necessarily implies that in these facts which

I find in my inmost life there is something greater than anything I can simply derive from myself, since I believe that they have a value in themselves and ought normally to compel every conscience. In other words, there are in fact no men who live completely outside a true and a false, a good and an evil. There are some who dispute this on an intellectual level, but by their conduct they belie what they profess on that level. That is why I insist on the importance of that demonstration of St. Augustine's, because that is precisely one of the aspects to which modern man is liable to be blind, because of one of the elements which he most seriously lacks. I mean that one of the most threatened things in modern man is precisely the intellect, trust in the intellect's power to enable us to know the real. The intellect has become an instrument of curiosity or erudition, of enjoyment and culture. But it has lost its dignity of being that by which we know reality in what it is.

Here, therefore, we have come to a point on which Christians of today really must reflect. The values of redemption must not make us underestimate the values of creation. We have to apply the fundamental value of creation, which God has said is good, equally to the order of thought. Herein lies the dignity of philosophy and metaphysics in the eyes of the Church. Philosophical thought is not merely the history of philosophy, nor is it reduced simply to the human sciences, as is often the case in our modern universities. It remains—and if Christians were the last to testify to this, they will remain its last witnesses—one of the highest disciplines of the intellect, that which enables us to attain with certainty to a realm which exceeds that of sensible experience as made known to us through the sciences. There is nothing more absurd in modern thought than to believe that the only certainties are those of the physical, chemical, or biological order. In the first place, these are never certainties but only hypotheses, and in the second place, if there were no certainties but these we should be certain only of what is not interesting; there would be no certainty about what is really interesting.

As I have said, in the end there are two things which are really interesting: others, and God. In the end the only interesting things are personal relations with our fellow men and women, and personal relations with God. These are the only things which concern the essentials of existence. Man would really be an absurd animal (and Sartre would be right in saying he is absurd) if he were prodigiously endowed for doing what is not interesting and totally unprovided for what is interesting. In that case it would be true that man is a monster, if for the essential things he found himself faced with the absurd, and adapted only for what is connected with a certain immediate arrangement of existence, which does not concern the ultimate problems.

That is why the problems I am raising here depend on these fundamental attitudes to existence. It is clear that when these attitudes are radically falsified from the start it is absolutely impossible to arrive at any solution. But we are in no way forced to be imprisoned in the absurd. That does not in any way constitute the normal human condition, provided we sincerely analyze its elements.

FROM LOVE TO LOVE

But we can start from the experience of beauty or of goodness, as well as from that of truth. We say that something is good, or that something is beautiful. But when I say that this is beautiful, I refer, in the very judgment I make, to beauty as something which exists in itself, and in which this object participates in a certain way. When I say, for example, that this sunset is beautiful, I am stating a relation between this landscape before my eyes and something in my mind which I call beauty. So, when I say: "How ugly this picture is," I speak in reference to something. Long ago, St. Augustine and St. Thomas reflected on this and said that all beauty participates in something of that which is beauty in itself, that is, in a certain objective reality to which I thus refer all reality, in order to establish a relation between it and what I call beauty. But beauty as such is limitless; beauty is not the beauty of some object, of some landscape, just as intelligence is not the intelligence of some person: it is something independent of all these varied participations to which I refer it.

Hence St. Augustine, and later St. Thomas, reach this conclusion, that all beauty, all goodness, all value, are thus necessarily participations in a reality in which beauty, goodness, and value are actualized in their fullness. Otherwise, when I state a relation between beauty and some particular beauty, my words would mean nothing, and there would be no content in the judgment I form. It is in fact true, and something we continually experience, that no beauty corresponds, for us, to "beauty." In other words, everything we meet by which we are enraptured creates a longing in us. Love, for example, arouses in us a longing which is not satisfied. I mean that there is much more in the fact of loving than any particular woman can give us. There is much more in aesthetic experience than the actual work of art which gave rise to it. When I come out from hearing a Bach sonata, I feel an infinite longing; the sonata has aroused in me the sense of beauty, but it cannot exhaust for me all the content of what it has awakened.

This is how creatures are signs, and finally, that is what the degrees of being signify. Every creature is a sign; it creates in me a nostalgia for something it cannot give me. "The world is a book in which everything speaks of God." And it is true that in this sense the great emotions in some way convert us, by coming to awake in us, through a particular reality, a certain thirst for the absolute—for torpor is the worst thing of all, and that is why music has a spiritual value. The value of creatures is that they transmit these messages to us and stir up in us that spiritual upheaval which opens us anew to the infinite. This is just what Claudel saw so clearly in *The Satin Slipper*. It is often love that performs this rôle. Sometimes this may be almost its only meaning: that is, there may be a love which humanly speaking cannot be satisfied, but has its full value through the inner upheaval it has stirred up in one who without it would have been mediocre. From this aspect, love in the "romantic" sense, the sense which Denis de Rougemont criticized in *L'amour et l'occident,* is none the less justifiable. Its justification is that there is a value in love *qua* love, that is, as a reflection of absolute love. Love has two senses: it is that which will unite the man and the woman, but also it is that by which, for the man through the woman, and for the woman through the man, the heart discovers what love is. That is why it is so often the occasion of the discovery of God, and that is only natural, just because it makes me touch an absolute value, with a kind of sweeping, dazzling evidence. In this sense, what I attain in that way surpasses anything a creature can ever give me, although the creature may be the means and the way by which I thus find God, and may be, as it were, a sign of him, a kind of sacrament. In this sense we can say that there is a kind of sacrament of love.

You see how, here again, we come on something which is not in the least an abstract process, but penetrates still further into the depths of being, yet can perfectly well be considered as intellectually accurate, so that I could say that this absoluteness of love which love enables me to discover is not some absurd, romantic dream; on the contrary, it is far more real than what is meant by those who believe that these touches of the absolute are illusions and that reality is necessarily sordid. You see what this involves: that the most real is also the most beautiful. That is the choice represented by belief in the existence of God. The opposite choice is to say that the most beautiful is necessarily illusion, there is nothing real but the sordid. One may think this. But to think this is to be false to the genuine witness of the heart, and it is not necessarily to be on the side of the intellect. It is perhaps one of the worst perversions of the intellect in our age that it identifies itself with destructive criticism, whereas, when it is really itself and used in all its nobility, it is precisely that which enables us to attain to the reality of things.

FROM THAT WHICH IS TO HIM WHO IS

But what I have been saying about truth, beauty, and goodness can be applied to all reality. We are in a world in which everything moves; that is, passes from something which it did not have to something more; in other words, it perpetually acquires value, for that is what movement is. It is not simply local movement but qualitative movement, far more. Everything, then, develops. Now, starting from this very elementary observation, St. Thomas asks this question: how can anything pass from a less to a more? When something was lacking, how can that something appear? Can the more be derived from the less? From the absence of something can one derive its appearing? And this perpetual passing "from potency to act" (to use the technical expression borrowed by St. Thomas from Aristotle), this process of perfecting and passing to a more—does it not imply that the "more" exists somewhere? For in fact the coming-into-existence of something implies some sort of intervention. Now it is not I who am the source of that more, it is not I who am the source of the existence of the value. In some way, therefore, the more must be prior to the less, if the less is to approach the more. In other words, from non-existence there can never come existence. For existence to spring from what does not exist, existence must first *be*, the more must first exist.

This leads to the fundamental statement that the point of departure is not the nothing, but being, and what is original is fullness. That is a tremendous and magnificent statement, which we have met on other levels. It means that beauty and goodness are being itself, that the real is fullness, and when we say that God exists, that is exactly what we are stating. We participate in this fullness in a deficient manner, but it is that fullness which is the reality. It means, in other words, that being is not, as with Sartre, that absurd opaqueness on which I dash myself: being, the very foundation of things, is, on the contrary, fullness of love, fullness of beauty, and fullness of joy. And it is precisely because reality itself is that, that I can participate in it and gradually be opened to it. Here we have a first consideration which is perfectly intelligent and perfectly logical, so long as one is not tied down to analyzing the relations between phenomena, but reflects on the very condition of their existence.

A proof which is complementary to this is the proof from purpose. The starting point is not now the fact that for something to exist and, in particular, to acquire value, that value must exist first. It is the observed fact—when I consider movement and especially the total cosmic movement—which St. Thomas could not yet see fully, but which a man like Teilhard de Chardin can see better, namely, that throughout the whole history of cosmic evolution (of the inanimate world, the animate world, and the human world) there exists a sort of movement which is, as it were, intelligent and reaching out to something.

Here again, one can dispute it, one can perfectly well say: the world is only an absurd comedy, everything is completely meaningless and is going nowhere. But a man like Teilhard, speaking as both a scientist and a philosopher, replies that we have no right to say this, for it is contrary to the real, contrary to the *data* of science and to serious reflection on science. We have no right to say whatever we like, not because of any external restraint, but because there are factual *data* which our intellect must first accept. And it is just this idea, that one can think what one likes, which is one of the things most opposed to the reality of the life of the intellect, which obliges us to take account of certain *data*.

Now this sort of magnetization of the cosmic movement in its totality tends in a certain direction, the direction of deepening, the direction of the more complex, and finally in the direction of the mind and of love, as constitutive elements of the person. Inasmuch as one starts from the inanimate world and, passing through the animate world, arrives at the world of the mind, it is clear that here is something which has a direction. But where exactly can the person go if not toward a personal universe? If it is indeed the reality of the person which emerges as the point of convergence of the whole cosmic movement, this is because what is supremely real is that personal reality, and at the pole of attraction of all that movement we can see, with Teilhard, the Omega point which is personal life in its fullness, and it is precisely this which we call God. If the whole cosmic movement is not magnetized by something which gives it its direction, movement is totally deprived of meaning. In that case it is quite impossible to understand how that movement reveals an order.

Ultimately we are led to start from existence itself. That is, the point of departure is an absolutely elementary fact, that to exist is something different from being some thing. For example, a flower exists, yet to exist is not even part of its definition as a flower, which consists simply of a certain number of qualities. Similarly, for a man, to exist does not form part of his actual essence. The essence of a man is to be a being composed of soul and body, with a certain number of properties, but the fact of existing does not form part of his actual essence, from which we deduce that in all that exists there are two things to be considered: first, that which it is— what is called its essence—and second, the fact that it exists.

Now, it is precisely from this fact of existing that the mind begins to reflect. It asks itself: what does it mean to exist; what is this absolutely prime and yet mysterious reality, which is not the same as being some thing, but is added to what any particular thing is? On the one hand to exist is some- thing absolutely real. Consequently we have here a point of departure which is certain, for if there is one thing of which we are certain it is our existence. This is disputed by Des- cartes, who said: "It is because I think that I know I exist," and not "It is because I am sure I exist that my thoughts acquire a meaning." But no matter! This is connected with a later step. The important thing is to start from the first fact, this reality of existing, and to note that it is not part of the essence of anything, but is yet something supremely real. Therefore there must be a being whose existence itself is its essence, a being which is existence, the act of existing. That is, to exist must be the property of a level, of a domain, ulti- mately of a being. In reality this argument is, after all, that employed by St. Thomas. Gilson has clearly shown that the thought of St. Thomas is essentially an existentialism, inas- much as he started from the particular existence to reach the absolute existence. That is to say, then, that finally, beyond all the particular forms of existing, there is that mysterious reality which is "existing" itself, and this is clearly a supreme order of reality, beyond everything, and ultimately the source of everything. Here philosophical thought really attains the very foundation of what is called ontology, the science of *being,* but of being understood as existing being, as it is real. Here we reach the very foundation of reality. As I have often remarked, the Christian revelation comes in to open out a final and supreme stage by showing that this "existing," which is in practice the ultimate ground of every being, is a personal "existing," and even tri-personal; absolute being, absolute existing, is love, and in this sense love and the absolute are found to be ultimately the same thing.

But this is a step to which only the Christian revelation introduces us. What metaphysics can by itself establish, in a step which is absolutely grounded and solid, is that, beyond all particular forms of existence, there is an absolute form of existence, which is the source of existence for all that exists. That is, that of myself I can give account of *what* I am, but not of the fact that I exist. My existence is something that is given me. There is therefore a source of existence. By this I mean that my essence gives account of what I am, in what is part of its actual definition: to be a man, to have understanding, a heart, a body, but not of that ultimate reality that this essence actually exists. Here we really touch what ontology is, that is, the supreme form of thought when it attains the reality of "existing" in its ultimate foundation, which is the very fact of being real, of being placed in existence. I do not exist in virtue of what I am, but what I am exists, because it is given to it to exist.

Here we clearly reach a fundamental experience. I am not my own source of existence, and nothing is its own source of existence, yet it is certain that I exist. It is certain that I exist, and it is certain that I am not by myself the reason for my existence. Yet it must be that the fact of my existence has its root somewhere and in something which is of the order of existence itself, that is, which accounts for the fact that I exist in the actual order of existence, in the fact of being placed in reality. It is in this sense that God here appears to us ultimately as the absolute reality, in which every reality participates in a restricted manner.

Let us note that the characteristic of the argument which enables us to ascend to God is precisely that it starts from existing reality, not simply from a logical necessity. It is a reflection on my existence and on the conditions of my existence. This, of course, may be neglected; I can be content with the order of secondary facts and causes. But if I am, I dissolve the problem in a series of secondary entanglements and never penetrate to its roots. Penetrating those roots makes me change my level and rise from the plane of merely contingent things to what gives them their reason and justification, and that is why the existence of God impels acceptance from every mind which honestly recognizes that which is, and correctly reflects on that given fact.

CHAPTER V

THE DIVINE PERFECTIONS

In our search for God we must never separate the inner process, the meeting with the personal God, from the speculative knowledge. If we are unable to base our beliefs on intellect and reason, we are likely to regard them as subjective things, for which we could not give account to others. In company with all the Church's tradition we believe that the intellect, even left to the light of reason and without revelation, is a creature of God, that God made it to know reality, and therefore that it is capable of knowing reality at its different levels: at the level of knowledge of the material world, which is science: at the level of relations with persons, which is the knowledge of others, and finally, beyond that, at the level of what surpasses the world of creation, which is the knowledge of God.

So far I have spoken only of the first aspect of that question, namely, whether God exists. We now come to another question, which in fact is often the one to raise most problems, the question, not only whether God exists, but whether we can know something about what he is. Can we know not only his existence but also his nature? This raises one of the most fundamental problems in the whole history of philosophy, one which is of great present relevance, the problem of what is called "negative theology" and "affirmative theology." Can we know anything about God except that he is nothing of what we know? Would not the claim to say anything about him be precisely to assimilate him to what he is not?

THE HIDDEN GOD

Let us first state the two terms of the question. Here we have two statements, each of which seems equally well founded. The first danger is what may broadly be called anthropomorphism. It consists, when we speak of God, in representing him in the manner of what we are ourselves. As has been well said, in this case it is not man who is made in the image of God, but God who is made in the image of man. This is a very real danger. We have already seen it on the level of the popular and spontaneous representations. Men will represent God by projecting onto a higher level the attitudes they are used to meeting on the human level. This can and often does result in distortions of the idea of God. It is therefore clear from the outset that we must begin by criticizing false ideas of God.

Very often what atheists criticize—and which they are right to criticize—is this type of representation. The weakness of atheism is to choose, in order to attack them, religious attitudes which religious men are the first to reject as absolutely spurious. It is easy to demolish a God whom one has first fashioned in such a way that he does not bear criticism. To think of God as only the equivalent on a higher level of the father in the family, the boss in the factory, the ruler in the state, as one, that is, who simply derives from a subordination of the lower to the higher, is to project onto God things which are true on the human level, but are quite different in God. This must first be criticized. From this point of view certain of the atheists' criticisms have some value as regards certain representations of God, but none as regards the real conception of him taught by the great Christian and non-Christian philosophers.

At a more advanced level there are certain representations of God of a more philosophical nature, but in them too God is still a projection of the human mind. This is the case, for example, with Voltaire's "watchmaker" God, who sets the great cosmic machine in motion, and is conceived on the model of an inventor of some sort of apparatus. This God merely seems necessary to explain a certain movement in the universe, but has none of the profound qualities which belong to God. The intellect is clearly tempted to extend the realities of this world into a higher world, but this still belongs to the order of created things, of which it is simply a higher form. The ancient philosophers had great difficulty in avoiding this temptation. The God of the Stoics, that fire which animates the universe and is its inner, vital principle, has no transcendence to offer. This is also, in this respect, the God of India, who ultimately represents simply the spirit in its highest form, so that in proportion as we purify the life of the spirit in ourselves, we end by identifying ourselves with that God, who is really nothing else but ourselves. Once again there is a danger of making God in the image of man, and thus offering, as object for our adoration, something which is really an idol, that is, a product of our mind.

All through the Christian tradition we find a ruthless criticism of these anthropomorphisms. The criticism is coextensive with the tradition. It appears already in the origins of Christianity, and before Christianity in the first inspired philosophers of the Bible, who at first were the Jews. The great tradition, which runs from the beginning of our era to the fourteenth century, and is that of the inspired metaphysics of the Bible, comprises three branches. There is the Jewish branch, beginning with Philo of Alexandria, and whose greatest representative is Maimonides in the twelfth century. There is a Moslem branch, for medieval Islam was penetrated by Greek philosophy, and there was an epoch of Mediterranean culture when it was the Moslems who provided the succession in transmitting Greek philosophical culture. Finally there is the Christian branch, represented by the Fathers of the Church and culminating in the thirteenth century with the great medieval doctors.

From the beginning, criticism of anthropomorphism in all its forms has been an essential theme, because the God of the Christians and the Jews and the Moslems is a transcendent God, one who is absolutely of a different order from all that exists in the world. As a consequence, the statement that God is different from all that we know, and that the first thing we know about him is that he is nothing of what we know, has been a fundamental theme from the beginning. Philo the Jew, whom I mentioned just now, in his wonderful commentary on the ascent of Moses on Sinai, represents Moses in the darkness where God dwells, as signifying that "the true knowledge of God is to know that we do not know him," that is, that here the true knowledge is to recognize our ignorance. This theme runs all through theology and mysticism. An English mystic of the middle ages wrote a book called *The Cloud of Unknowing*. The theme of the divine night is essential in St. John of the Cross: "The Dark Night." All this is connected with the fundamental idea that to attain the reality of God, we must go beyond all images and concepts, for the reality of God is far above all the concepts that we can form of him. Nothing could be more dangerous than to identify God with what we say about him, which means that whenever we say anything about God we must both affirm it and deny it. When I say: "God is good," I must at once add: "God is not good"; that is, the goodness of God is something other than what we call "goodness." It is not alien to what we call goodness, but it is something completely different from what we call good. This is what purifies our idea of God from everything we might put into it which could be simply the expression of what we are ourselves.

This attitude, which begins with Philo, is represented in the patristic age chiefly by the great theologian of the negative theology, Gregory of Nyssa. In his *Life of Moses* he describes the ascent of Moses as an image of the ascent of the soul, which rises gradually into the darkness where God dwells, and is united to God in the night of faith. St. Thomas Aquinas, one of the great doctors of the knowledge of God, who will tell us in a moment that we can know something of God, begins his *Summa theologiae* with this double affirmation, that we can say everything about God, but that we must also deny everything about God. It is essential, he explains, to get beyond univocal knowledge, which applies a concept to God in the same sense as to a creature, and take up the position of analogy, as the philosophers call it, that is, the knowledge of a certain relation between the goodness of God and the goodness of creation, which is still only a relation.

This attitude can be carried very far, and has been so carried in contemporary philosophy. It may be true that at the moment we are faced rather with an exaggeration of this attitude. One of the men who has laid most stress on the negative theology is the great Calvinist theologian Karl Barth. Barth's great idea, which we meet in modern Protestantism, especially among young Protestants, is that all the ideas we can form of God through our reason are deluding, and that a rational knowledge of God can only lead us into error. The only way to the knowledge of God is revelation; only Jesus Christ causes us to know God. The attempts of the religions and the philosophies to form an idea of God only result in the forging of an idol. In other words, only God can tell us what he is. If it is man who speaks of God, what he says is necessarily false. Certain representatives of this school are tempted nowadays to exalt atheism, as they see in it a denial of the whole idea of God, and make it out to be a purifying process which is the necessary condition for discovering the true God, the God who manifests himself only through faith. The exclusive accent placed on this aspect, and the exaggerated forms it assumes, constitute a danger, and all the more because it finds support in the scientific spirit.

Scientific men are led by the very methods which belong to science to separate the domain of the intellect, which for them is expressed in the rigor of the laws of science, from the domain of faith, which concerns a quite different order. Philosophical arguments bore them, insofar as, in their view, these are a use of the intellect which has not the rigor they find in the scientific disciplines. For a man of science it is easier to adhere to the God of faith, the God who is the subject only of a personal relation, than to the God of the intellect, who is reached by the processes of reason. Thus it is now widely doubted whether the intellect can attain to metaphysics, both by certain existentialists and by certain positivists. The recent educational reforms almost completely suppress the teaching of philosophy, which used to be the culmination of secondary studies in France, and replaces it with the human sciences, such as political economy and scientific psychology. In France there is now a danger that philosophy will disappear from education, and this is a sort of index of the massive evolution of the modern world toward the scientific subjects, and of a disaffection toward the higher forms of study, philosophical and metaphysical. This is an abdication of the intellect in its highest functions and ambitions.

THE KNOWN GOD

That is why, having said—as all Christian philosophy has said—that we cannot form for ourselves an idea of God which corresponds accurately to what he is, and that we must therefore deny all that we say about God, we must now add the counterbalance. What I have been saying does not mean that we cannot know anything about God or that what we say about him is untrue. The whole problem is here, in that equilibrium between the two poles of anthropomorphism and agnosticism. It is false to say that we know God as he is, for that would be anthropomorphism, making God in our own image, but it is equally false to say that we know nothing about God, for that would be agnosticism, which ends by saying that in fact, in practice, God may perhaps exist, but in any case we are sure of only one thing, that we know absolutely nothing about him.

Against this position the Christian philosophers, and St. Thomas in particular, have always affirmed that we can know something about God by the analogy of created things, that is, that everything we say about him is both true and false. To take the example of God's goodness; when I say that God is good, this is false, because the goodness of God is absolutely different from all that I mean by the word goodness. Yet this is true, for it is true that there exists in God something which corresponds in an eminent degree to what I call goodness. The goodness of creatures can give me a certain idea of what God's goodness is, on condition that I do not identify it with that goodness, for if I do, I shall make an over-simple image of God's goodness which would identify it with goodness in the order of created things. Similarly, when I say that God is beautiful, it is perfectly true that God is the very splendor of beauty, but it is also true that the glory of God has no relation to what in fact I call beauty in the aesthetic sense of the word. If I confuse the two levels, I give myself an idea of God which devalues him, by assimilating him to the realities of my common experience. We find this already in the Bible. The book of Job says, about the marvels of the world: "Lo, these are but the outskirts of his ways; and how small a whisper do we hear of him! But the thunder of his power who can understand?" If the beauty of the world gives me an idea of God, what he is in reality is of such intensity that I could not bear it. No man can see God and live. If I cannot know God as he is, it is not because he is unreal: rather it is because the intensity of his existence, the density of his being, is such that my feelings and my understanding could not possibly bear it. St. John of the Cross called God "darkness," because his light is so dazzling that in a way it burns up our sight.

Thus we reach this paradoxical statement, that everything we say about God is false, and at the same time it is true. In his *Treatise on the Divine Names* Pseudo-Dionysius says:

> Thus, taught, the theologians all together praise God, for having no name, and for possessing all names. For having no name; for they recall that the thearchy itself, in one of those mystical visions in which it is symbolically represented, rebuked him who asked: "What is your name?" And to deter him from all knowledge which could be expressed by a name, it spoke thus: "Why is it that you ask my name?" He is Wonderful. And they praise him for having many names, since he next wills to describe it, saying of itself (*sc.* the thearchy): "I am who am," or again: "I am the life; I am the light; I am God; I am the truth." Then they say that this divine principle belongs to intellects, to souls, and to bodies, that it is altogether identical in the identical, at the heart of the universe, around the universe, beyond the universe, sun, star, earth, fire, spirit, dew, cloud, absolute rock, stone: in a word, all that which is, and nothing of that which is.

This passage shows that everything we say of God is true, that is, when we denote him by material objects and when, like the Bible, we call him a rock, a star, a dew, a water, a stone, because in fact, if everything comes from God, everything has a certain reflection of God, everything gives us an idea of God. And now we reverse our position of a moment ago. It is true that for a man who can read the meaning behind the world, the whole world is a book which speaks of God. All creatures tell us something about God. The world of nature and the world of man tell us something about God, because everything comes from him and everything is a reflection of him.

This second affirmation thus acts as a corrective to the purely negative aspect of the first. When I say that God is dew, or light, or rock, I am clearly not identifying him with a spring, a ray, or a stone. But on the other hand I do say something, and what I say is true. There is something in God which corresponds to the solidity of a rock, the brilliance of the light, or the refreshing of the dew. The mystics, who have a realistic understanding, and prefer images to concepts, help us through those images, perhaps more profoundly than through the concepts, to grasp the reality of the matter directly, as it were, in an intuition. If I say that God is a rock, I say something which in some respects is stronger in its impact on me than if I say that God is immovable. The abstraction deprives the image of a certain intensity of suggestion. We can quite easily pass from one register to the other, we can use either an image or a concept. In fact we have to pass from the concrete experience to its more abstract formulation. The truth remains that through all the realities of the world and of man, we can ascend to God, and therefore there is no impassable abyss between God and created things. God is transcendent and absolutely above all things, yet it is true, as Pseudo-Dionysius says, that he is equally immanent; he is present in all things.

God is both the most known and the most unknown. There is something in God which is known. God is perhaps the one we know best. A little child already knows God, perhaps before he can recognize father or mother, because the consciousness of God is rooted in the depths of the human soul. At the same time the greatest mystics tell us that they do not know God. St. John of the Cross calls him "the Unknown Islands," for God is always beyond all that we can grasp, and yet all that we can grasp really tells us something about him.

Hence the knowledge of God is a perpetual growing and a perpetual surpassing. "To find God," said Gregory of Nyssa, "is to seek him without ceasing." The knowledge of God consists in growing perpetually in the discovery of the inexhaustible. It is perfectly true that we know God and that we advance in that knowledge. At the same time it is true that we shall never exhaust that knowledge, that God will always be, in his reality, beyond all that we can grasp of him. Man's destiny is an awe-struck discovery of ever-new riches. If God is indeed the infinite abyss, eternity itself will not suffice for us to reach his limits, and, to quote again from Gregory of Nyssa, the soul will eternally "go from beginning to beginning, by beginnings which have no end." The utmost peak of the knowledge of God in a great mystic is still only a starting point in comparison with what remains to be known. What we grasp of God, we grasp really, and that is really something of him. But what our mind knows at a given moment is always infinitely lacking in comparison with what he is and with what we still have to know about him.

But the question then arises: if eternity itself is still only an eternal search, can we ever be satisfied? It is a disturbing thought, that our life can be without rest forever. But we might feel an opposite sort of anxiety at the idea that our life will one day be a rest, for in fact we are so made that we desire both the possession and the search, and we cannot decide which we prefer; we don't know whether we prefer the rest or the movement. To this Gregory of Nyssa replies that beatitude is the eternal synthesis of both; beatitude, by filling up the measure of what we can receive, widens our capacity and makes us capable of new riches. Thus we shall eternally be satisfied to the measure of our capacity, but our capacity will continually grow, yet we shall always be open to new things.

Thus there can be a truth of the knowing of God, and at

the same time a truth of his "unknowing." The unknowing is not a denial of the knowing, but an affirmation that the object known far transcends all that we can know about it. One can very really both know God and never know him completely. That is to say that our knowledge will never be comprehensive, to use the technical term. By comprehensive knowledge we mean that which exhausts its object. It is obvious that if we could "exhaust" God we should be God himself. As St. John of the Cross so well expresses it, we shall always be disciples in relation to God. We shall always have to receive. God's relation to us will eternally be that of a transcendence to what is transcended. But it does not mean at all that the participation in him to which we are called is not, for all that, a real participation, and one all the more capable of expanding without end, because never, I repeat, can it equal that to which it aspires. That is beyond all that can ever be attained.

Here we arrive at that synthesis which is so difficult and which so few philosophies have discovered. It safeguards the absolute transcendence of God. What makes God to be God, in fact, is that he is "the wholly other," that he is other than all that we can know about him. Yet this statement is compatible with that other statement, that already, on the plane of our rational intelligence, we can know something about him through that creation which is his image, and sing his praises. Even more, in Christ he makes us sharers in that very knowledge with which he knows himself. For faith is a sharing in the very knowledge with which God knows himself, so that we are capable of advancing ever further in that eternal discovery of the wonders of God.

I shall speak later of the knowledge of faith, but I would add that here we again find the statement that man is already, in himself, in his nature, a being made for God, and therefore capable of entering into relations with him. It is essential to repeat this, for it is true for every age. But the problem of our time is precisely how to find which are the ways to the knowledge of God through modern man's experience of the world and of himself. Everything can lead us to God and everything speaks of him, but that book has still to be deciphered. Now too often we speak of God through the experience of the man of yesterday, and so the witness we bear does not touch the man of today: our theology and our symbolism are still tied to an obsolete experience. Therefore the task of Christians is to decipher the divine meaning of contemporary civilization, to show that there is no reason why it should close man in on himself, that it is as capable as any other of opening man to God. But the question is: have Christians enough imagination, enough creative invention, to extend it and surpass it by a religious experience?

THE UNION OF CONTRARIES

In our study of the philosophical knowledge of God, after speaking of God's existence, we considered whether we could know anything about him, and in that connection I said that when our subject is the knowledge of God, we must always make two complementary statements. On the one hand, everything speaks to us of God, and as Pseudo-Dionysius said in the text I quoted: he is both "all that which is, and nothing of that which is." On the other hand, whenever we say anything about God, we must always state the denial of that thing, lest we represent God in the image of the things of this world. In this sense, as Origen said, it is always dangerous to speak about God, meaning that whenever we speak about God we are cruelly aware how everything we say about him is deficient, compared with what he is. To the extent that we have glimpsed something of his glory and splendor, we feel the absolute impotence of words to express what we feel. It is the same with the more intense human experiences; we feel how deficient our language is, compared with the experience and its fullness. This is supremely true when we speak of that highest domain of experience, that of our meeting with God.

Particularly, when we speak of God, must we avoid placing him in a special category. That is one of the aspects of God's transcendence in relation to all reality. And it is no doubt one of the most important, for it is one of those in which we run the greatest risk of giving a false image of God. Let me give a few examples of this. It is common practice to speak of God's greatness, and indeed, when we say that God is great, we mean something. We mean that, in an absolutely eminent and transcendent way, he represents all that is connected with greatness in the human sphere. This is true of greatness in the spatial sense, that which constitutes the actual immensity of creation. We mean that God is infinitely greater than the totality of the universe as far as we can see it. It is true also in a moral sense; the greatness of God is incomparable in relation to all that we call most great in the world, in the greatness of genius, of character, of the intellect.

But this statement must at once be corrected by another. Paradoxical as it may appear, we must at once add that God is little. Pseudo-Dionysius, in that *Treatise on the Divine Names* which I have called the most wonderful treatise in existence on God, wrote this: "The Scriptures praise God as great and under the mode of greatness, but they also speak of the divine littleness, which is revealed in a gentle breath." If greatness expresses an aspect of reality, littleness—what Pascal called "the infinitely little," and which modern science is helping us to discover—is also an aspect of reality. To place God only under the category of greatness, and not also under the category of littleness, would be to place him in one category of being, to relate him to only one part of reality, whereas he is precisely the one in whom absolutely all reality finds its eminent expression. This is important on the human level. Insofar as we emphasize only God's greatness, we give the impression that he is infinitely remote from everything in us which is, precisely, littleness. Now there is a divine littleness, an aspect of divinity which is infinitely near to the little and the humble. It is also in this sense that God is both all that is most exterior and all that is most interior. When we speak of the greatness of God, we put all the accent on the fact that he infinitely surpasses us and is infinitely remote from us. Now, as St. Augustine said so truly: "God is also he who is in me, more myself than I," *intimior intimo meo,* more interior to myself than myself. God surpasses me on all sides. I can look for him in what is outside me, but I can also look for him in what is inside me. He surpasses me both by the infinite greatness which is revealed to me in creation, and by the infinite intimacy by which, when I turn in on myself and on my innermost self, and finally in that source from which my own inmost being perpetually emanates, I find him again. To fail to recognize that aspect of God's interiority, to see God only under his exterior aspect, is to miss the fullness of what he is.

To take another example: the first definition of the Catechism, as I learned it when I was a child—but so many things change in the Church that the Catechism is changed too— was that God is a pure spirit, eternal and sovereign master of all things. (What God is in the latest Catechism I don't know, but I stick to that definition.) But I maintain that the definition seems dangerous. When I say that God is pure spirit, I give the impression of contrasting God with the world of matter. To define God as spirit is to place him in the order of intellectual realities, and therefore to suggest that material things are alien to him. In this definition there is even a hint of scruple, since it says not only that God is spirit, but that he is *pure* spirit, and by that addition we seem to mean that he is utterly free from anything resembling matter. Now this is false, for if God possesses in an eminent degree the qualities of all existing things, it is obvious that in matter, which is God's creature, there are qualities possessed eminently by God. We often find that nonbelievers think Christians to be idealists or spiritualists (not, of course, in the current English sense, but in the sense that they are on the side of the spirit and against matter). And as modern men are for the most part chiefly engaged in investigating matter through science, and in utilizing matter by technology, they have the impression that Christianity belongs to a world which is foreign to their interests. That is one of the reasons why so many of them feel that there is a gulf between them and Christianity. But this gulf has nothing to do with Christianity's true nature, being caused by the false image too often given by Christianity of itself. For the truth is that a Christian is no more a "spiritualist" than a materialist, and we must emphasize the fact that there is such a thing as a Christian materialism, not in the sense that for the Christian everything can be reduced to matter (which would be the inverse error to favoring only the spirit), but in the sense that matter is something perfectly valuable, one of the expressions of God's creation, so that through it we can grasp something of God, as we can through the spirit.

What characterizes God is not that he is immaterial, but that he is supermaterial: that, in the order of what matter is, he is infinitely more intense than matter. It is not that he is foreign to it but rather that he expresses its intensity in its highest form. And that is precisely why Pseudo-Dionysius said that God is not only spirit, beauty, and light, but also sun, rock, or star, choosing thus a certain number of images borrowed from the world of matter, to teach us that these material things too give us an idea of God. In other words, God can be reached both through ideas and through images. And if God can be reached through images, it is because those images really express something of him. They are what I called, earlier in this book, the "hierophanies," explaining that the visible speaks to us of God, because it really represents a certain reflection of his splendor. The beauty of a sunset or of a mountain landscape arouses in us a genuine sense of the sacred, because these things really are a certain expression of what God is. It must at once be added in this connection that there is an ambiguity about the meaning of the word "spirit," which I have already emphasized, but we must constantly return to these elementary notions. The fact is that in a philosophical perspective of Greek origin the word spirit has a different meaning from what it has in a biblical perspective of Semitic origin. "Spirit" always has the idea of breath. But the point which the Greeks noted about breath was that it is a subtle kind of matter. It is in this sense that we speak of spirits of wine, spirituous liquors, that Descartes spoke of animal spirits, meaning material things. And it was from this idea of an infinitely subtle matter that the idea of breath came to mean that which is non-material. It is in this sense that men came to speak of "spiritualism" or "spiritism" (as opposed to materialism). We have a whole gamut of possible meanings in which, starting from a subtle material, "spirit" comes to denote the most subtle element in man, what we call the intellect, and the Greeks called *nous*.

To the Semites, however, "breath" evokes quite a different image, that of the storm, the tempest, irresistible power. It is in this sense that we call the Spirit "creative"—*Veni Creator spiritus*. The Spirit brooded over the primeval waters; that is, the irresistible power of God called things out of nothing. It is that Spirit who, on the day of Pentecost, in a rushing mighty wind which is a visible symbol of the Spirit's irruption, takes hold of the apostles to make them capable of doing things which are quite beyond human powers. The definition of the Spirit in the Bible is a divine power, making a carnal man able to accomplish "spiritual" things, which are absolutely beyond his own reach. It is in this sense that God is "spirit"

in the Bible, not in the sense of "spiritualism" or infinite
subtlety, but in the sense of irresistible power. It means that
the word signifies the infinite density and power of the divine
existence. It is needless to say what effects this has had in all
fields, including that of spirituality. Many errors arise from
confusing spiritualism with spirituality. Spirituality is not,
in fact, the Buddhist manner of developing the element of
interiority in us, in opposition to the way of materiality;
making ourselves somehow more and more immaterial, till
we become as it were translucid. To many people the ideal
of spirituality is to be somehow dematerialized, as we speak
of a coffee being decaffeinated: deprived, somehow, of its
materiality. To our contemporaries, a spiritual man is one
who is practically reduced to skin and bones!

This has nothing to do with what Christianity calls spirituality, which is simply what the Holy Ghost carries out in us.
It does not mean making the spirit dominate over matter, in
the sense of the intellectual over the material. It means being
made alive by the Holy Ghost in both body and soul. To become spiritual does not mean in the least to sacrifice the
body to the spirit, but to be gripped by the Holy Ghost in
soul and body. This is already done in this life by the Holy
Ghost in our soul, and spirituality means to live by the life
of the Holy Ghost, not to practice yoga! But there are still
many who confuse the two things. They see no difference between a Hindu and a Christian, between St. John of the Cross
and Shankara. To practice yoga, to make a meditation, it is
all one; they consist in recollecting oneself. This is a fundamental equivocation.

Christian spirituality is what the Holy Ghost performs
in us, and he is able to make us spiritual men in the very
midst of action. It is useless for a Christian "spiritual" to
retire from the world. The greatest Christian saints were engaged in the heat of action. But they were under the influence
of the Holy Spirit. On the other hand, that spirituality will

have eschatological repercussions on our body itself. This is the Christian dogma of the resurrection of the body, the statement, according to St. Paul, that we shall have spiritual bodies. For the "spiritualists" the expression is absurd, for to them a spiritual body would be a body which was no longer material, or rather, a sort of material body as unlike as possible to an actual material body: a sort of ghostly body deprived of all materiality. When I was a boy I had a drawing master who always drew his saints rather like ghosts. He gave the impression that having a body was something rather indelicate, and that a saint, therefore, was one who ought to have as little body as possible. But this is really nothing to do with Christianity. On the contrary, our glorious bodies will be more bodily than any we know. Not only will our bodies not be destroyed, they will instead be freed from all the slaveries in them which prevent them being fully actualized. Here we have a Christian optimism which lets us see, in the beauty of nature, in the beauty of the human body, something which will be called to transfiguration, not to destruction, and then all that really forms part of creation will be detached from all the limitations and dangers of its existence here.

So it is absurd to think that the development of science or technics, all that concerns us in the material world, cuts us off from God. But again it is the Christians who, from lack of imagination or from wrong thinking, don't know how to find God through matter. And, as I have already said here, this is precisely one of the great tasks of the evangelists of tomorrow's civilization. The problem is not only how to evangelize men but how to evangelize the world itself, that is, to see that the world becomes again that means of going to God which it is by nature. But there is a certain streak of Platonism, Jansenism, or Manichaeism lurking in many Christians, which prevents their having that genuinely Christian attitude.

To take another example: it is often said that God is unchangeable. That certainly expresses a truth. But also, for the modern man, this has something unattractive about it, insofar as life, for us, is in movement, and we cannot help associating the idea of unchangeableness with immobility. That idea of a God who is immobile, and of a beatitude which consists in sharing that immobility, gives us a sort of dread, and we wonder whether, when we are in that state of unchangeableness, we shall regret the good time when there was still movement. The prospect of that kind of beatitude does not seem very attractive. If on the one hand the idea of unchangeableness seems to guarantee stability—and there are times when we are tired of instability—on the other hand, in another sense, we have a sort of instinct that makes us feel that in movement there is an authentic expression of being.

For modern men in particular—one thinks, for example, of a philosopher like Bergson—it is clear that this seems self-evident. Here too it would be a mistake to place God only in the category of the unchangeable. For ultimately, "unchangeable" is only an image for us. We start from the stability of things, the immobility of a rock, for instance, and we say that in God there is something which corresponds to that unchangeableness and is a perfection. But on the other hand we cannot be blind to the value that there is in movement, and in the same way it would be absurd to exclude this from God.

This again is said in so many words by Pseudo-Dionysius: "God is stable and immobile, remaining always the same, and yet he is mobile, since he diffuses himself constantly through all things." The life of God is, then, a paradoxical synthesis, in which both the perfection of stability and the perfection of mobility coincide in a manner which to us is unimaginable, but which enables us to affirm that all the perfection of each exists eminently in God. Here again we touch a point which is important with modern men. How often I have heard this objection: "What worries me about faith is that once you have believed, all problems are solved, whereas what interests me is search. But once all the problems are solved, there is no more search."

To think that for a Christian all the problems are solved, that the Christian life is not always a search and will not always be a search (as St. Gregory of Nyssa so well said, in the passage I have quoted), is to give a false idea of the genuine Christian condition. It is, on the pattern of God, a fundamental stability, to the extent that it is no longer at the mercy of the doubt of what is acquired. Stability means that the things acquired are acquired forever. But on the other hand it is always progressing to ever new acquisitions, for we shall never exhaust the riches of God. But what constitutes stability is the impossibility of going backward. That is why stability, for the created mind, is a perpetual progress, which is the very synthesis of stability and movement, and that is the definition of progress. This is fundamental stability, for it always progresses from acquisition to acquisition in a continuous line, and at the same time it is perpetual movement, for it is perpetual acquisition. This is true, moreover, of all spiritual realities. That is why there is satiety of the flesh, but never of the mind. The mind is never wearied, for the genuinely spiritual realities, even at the level of human love, are a perpetual growth. It is only when we fall back to the level of the flesh that we meet satiety, for the law of what is carnal is satiety and alternation, whereas it is the very character of the mind that it can always progress, for the mind is inexhaustible.

If the mind of man is inexhaustible, if the person of another is inexhaustible, if we can never reach the boundaries of the one we love, how much more unlimited are the boundaries of the infinitely loved being! In the things which belong to the mind there are never any limits. The mind is by nature without frontiers; and in consequence this introduces into spiritual realities an element of progress and perpetual search. Here everything is only a beginning, and growth is always possible.

From these examples we can see how important it is never to place God in a category and to be careful, whenever we say anything about him, to correct what we say by the complementary affirmation. What precisely characterizes God is to possess eminently in himself all that exists in the order of creation. But it is precisely *all;* that is to say, that in no degree can he be placed in one category of existence. He absolutely transcends all the categories and possesses in himself all that can exist in every order of things.

Among the characteristics of God which man can establish by this intellectual search I shall quote only one more, because it presents a peculiar difficulty and is particularly important. It is that of personality. Very often today we meet the idea, as we have met it in the ancient philosophies, that the divine infinity is incompatible with personality, and that since God is infinite he cannot at the same time be personal. This is characteristic of the ancient philosophies. To the Indian mind, God is that which transcends all delimitation; now, personality is perceived as a certain delimitation, therefore God must be impersonal, or transpersonal. He will personalize himself in his manifestation, which the Hindus call "Ishwar," in such a way as to be able to put himself in relation with man. But the relation of man to God on a personal level will be seen to be inferior, and truly to attain God one must depersonalize oneself in order to lose oneself in the infinite impersonality. In us too the person is a limitation, and we must therefore rise above our personal being, so as to identify ourselves with the fundamental unity of all things. I emphasize this point, in which there are very often confusions, even among Christians. They conceive union with God, not as a union of person with person, remaining distinct in an exchange of love, but as a dissolution of our personal being in the divine infinity. This remains one of the difficulties of contemporary thought, the person seeming to be a contingent limitation, and reality to be the permanence of the laws of the universe, within which the destiny of individual persons seems of little account. This is because of a confusion between personality and individuality.

But in fact, more and more—and it must be said that this is a great achievement of modern thought—we are discovering the person under a quite different aspect, that of "value." Today we understand that the human person constitutes, in fact, the supreme value in the order of created things. Once the person appears under this aspect of value, and if God is precisely he in whom all realities exist in a transcendent manner, it would be unthinkable that this aspect of creation, which we see to be that which has the greatest value in the world, should not also exist in him in an eminent degree. In other words, the idea of an impersonal God becomes all the more unthinkable, if personality is precisely the supreme value. It is very true that, for us, personality implies limits. But this again shows how we must place God in the extension of what constitutes the values we find in the world and, at the same time, purify that representation from everything which, on the level of created values, prevents them being perfectly fulfilled.

If, when I say that God is a person, I attribute to him the behavior of human persons, it is too obvious that I fall into anthropomorphisms, which give a false idea of God. When I ascribe to God certain attributes which are those of the person, I must both state them and at the same time purify them of their limitations. To take an example, great as human fatherhood is, it is rarely free from certain limitations, from a certain authoritarianism, a certain paternalism, a certain spirit of domination. The consequence is that many make the mistake of imagining God the Father on the model of the fathers of this world. They end by making themselves a God in the image of man, and this God in the image of man is what they feel it a duty to reject when they grow up. Just as an adult has to free himself from his dependence on his human father, so, in a similar manner, if the Father of heaven is thought of in this way, there will have to be a similar kind of liberation. That is why we must be so careful in our handling of these categories. As I said, it is dangerous to speak about God. One can give a false idea of God, and often the atheists reject what is in reality this false idea. It is perfectly true that there exists in God what represents the valuable element in the idea of fatherhood, but at the same time, when I apply that expression to God, I must strip it of whatever represents the limitations which are those of all human fatherhood.

A final difficulty in connection with this knowledge of God is the difficulty of understanding—this is what Sartre and Merleau Ponty have expressed—how God and his creation can exist together. We must choose; either God exists and I do not, or I exist and God does not. Man can conquer his existence only by the death of God. This is Nietzsche's great theme, so often followed by contemporary atheism. The reality of the problem must not be minimized. It is indeed difficult to understand how God and his creation can coexist. The best-known example of this, which we shall never in fact be able fully to explain, is how God can be the cause of everything—which is what I affirm—and at the same time I can be absolutely free. Now, here we have two affirmations whose coexistence it is extremely difficult to conceive.

In a more general way, which is the point of view of many moderns, if everything already exists in God in an eminent manner, that is, if in God all the possibilities of existence are already exhausted, and in an absolutely transcendent manner, there is no more interest in anything. Because if everything has already existed in God, my existence consists only in very imperfectly repeating what has been very well done a first time. Once everything has already realized its perfection in God, what interest then remains in an existence which is no more than a necessarily deficient replica? Does this not rob the human adventure of all interest? If nothing really new can ever appear, since everything exists already and in a far better state, what interest can there be in human effort, in invention, in progress? This is what leads some contemporary thinkers, in their effort to reconcile the idea of God with the idea of progress, to place God, not at the beginning, but at the end. We may say that ultimately this is what appears in the great metaphysics of history. It is the very foundation of the thought of Hegel—I do not say of the thought of Marx, because for Marx there is no God. For Hegel the absolute spirit is the totalization, at the end, of all which will be constituted in the becoming. It is what Rilke said too in this quotation from the *Letters to a Young Poet*: "Why not think that God is he who will come, who from all eternity must come, that he is the future, the final fruit of a tree whose leaves we are? . . . Don't you see that whatever happens is a beginning? . . . What would be the meaning of our search if he whom we seek belonged already to the past?" Here we have a sort of divinization of the future.

Is there something insoluble about this mystery? It is true that the existence of God dispossesses and alienates us—for in the end that is what it involves—so that existence is found to be transferred to God and withdrawn from man? Here we meet a theme we have already encountered. The fact that man is a creature and therefore holds all that he has from God, does not dispossess man of existence, for man's existence is a real existence, his freedom is a real freedom, his creations are real creations. Our existence is still fully valid, fully creative, and therefore in no way deprived of its consistence. What it is dispossessed of, however, is its self-sufficiency. To many modern men it seems intolerable not to depend on oneself, not to be an absolute beginning, but to receive oneself from another. Now this desire to belong to oneself is not a value; on the contrary it is a denial of that which, in a Christian perspective, is essential to life; namely, that life always exists in exchange and communication. Again I repeat it in a word: this exists between men. We must gladly agree to live only in an exchange, in which we both receive and give. The refusal to give, like the refusal to receive, is a refusal to live. This exists too between us and God, for between God and us there is that exchange of grace and thanks. For us, to live is to receive ourselves from love and to bring ourselves back to love.

Finally, this exists in God himself, for the very foundation of the mystery of God in the Christian vision is that he does not consist in one solitary person but in three persons. In him, personal life exists in the form of a communion of persons. If in God himself personal life consists in a communion of persons who communicate themselves wholly to one another, it would be absurd if personal life on the human level consisted in depending only on oneself. And it is precisely because we are created in the image of the triune God that the fact of receiving ourselves in a gift, and so of living in an exchange, is not something which alienates our essence, but rather fulfills it completely. In this way the Christian conception of the Trinity ultimately expresses what we have already established on the plane of philosophical thought.

CHAPTER VI

THE GOD OF REVELATION

The manifestation of God is given at different levels, corresponding to different historical stages. The first revelation is that of which I have spoken so far; we may call it the cosmic revelation, representing God's revelation to every man, through the world and through conscience. This is what constitutes the element of truth in the nonbiblical religions, like Hinduism and the religions of China and Africa. As I have said, this was a genuine revelation of God, through which every man can know something about him, and it has two aspects, as it were: the one immediate, that of religious experience, and the other, that of philosophical reflection. Religious knowledge and philosophical knowledge are on the same level, the level of what is directly accessible to all men, and they correspond to two aspects of one and the same fact. One aspect is spontaneous and direct, the other is considered and acquired intellectually. We have seen, too, that this knowledge of God enables us to reach, in some way, only God's external aspect. It enables every man to know that God exists and also to know something about him by means of the created world, for since all things come from God, all things are a certain reflection of God, and in this way nature and man are images of God.

But apart from that, what God is in himself—what constitutes his "interiority," his inner life, his personality in the deepest sense of the word—is totally inaccessible to man's efforts. Every human attempt to penetrate the heart of the mystery of God is blocked by an insuperable obstacle: his transcendence. Between man and God there is a gulf fixed, which no man can cross. Consequently, man can only fully know God insofar as God crosses that gulf and manifests himself to him, and that is what is called revelation in the strict sense of the word. That revelation was given first, in the Old Testament, to the people of Israel, and then in the New Testament to the Christian people.

REVELATION

Herein lies the radical distinction between the religions and revelation. It is a point to which I have often returned, so I need only recall it in a word. The religions are the expressions of man's search for God; they are the creations of the human genius, which is why they are always tainted with imperfections, because in this groping search man mixes elements of truth with elements of error. The judgment we have to give on these non-Christian religions is therefore twofold. On the one hand we recognize in them the authentic expression of man as religious; they attest, as I have often said, that it is of the very nature of man that a part of his being should be turned to God. From this point of view atheism, by refusing to admit this dimension of man, betrays humanism, because it deprives man of an essential dimension of himself. That is why I hold any religion to be preferable to atheism.

But on the other hand, in this groping search, the image which men form of God by means of the various religions is always more or less tainted with anthropomorphism and those various deformations I have enumerated: pantheism, in which the border lines between God and man are blurred; idolatry, in which created things are taken for God himself; dualism, which posits two principles at the origin of things. And so it is that, as the Protestant theologian Emil Brunner has said, every religion contains both its profound truth and its profound error. Thus these various religious forms are always ambiguous. In the last resort, in fact, only God speaks of God; we cannot truly know God as he is, unless God himself manifests himself directly, for then the base and foundation of our knowledge is no longer the groping search of man but the actual authority of God.

A little reflection will show that it is natural for it to be so, that is, that we can only know the inner life of God by revelation, for this is true even on the level of human relations. Since God is personal, he is necessarily mysterious, inaccessible. Our intellect by itself can never know anything about persons except what can be objectified. Even at the human level, the "interiority" of the human person is absolutely inaccessible. We cannot penetrate the secrets of the heart. God alone can plumb the heart's depths. So long, then, as we stop short at a knowledge of others which derives from what is accessible to us—that is, from their external appearance or visible aspect—the very essence of the other remains hidden from us. We can know the other only if he reveals himself to us, and that revelation is always something voluntary; he can perfectly well refuse to reveal himself to us, and he will reveal himself to us only in mutual trust, in the loving will to give himself to us by making us free of the intimacy of his person. That is what happens in friendship, that is what happens in love, in which we really penetrate into that mysterious world of the heart of the other, which otherwise remains completely closed to us. We can never gain its intimacy by any sort of breaking in. That is precisely what constitutes the person: to be a depth, an inaccessible abyss, unlike anything which can be grasped by science. As soon as we rise in the hierarchy of things, scientific knowledge becomes useless, for it can only reach the visible and the external, and we are obliged to enter on another mode of access to the truth, which is testimony, speech, that by which the other, in a free gift, reveals himself to us.

We must emphasize this, because it is one of the delusions of a certain type of contemporary intelligentsia to believe that scientific knowledge is the very type of all knowledge. Science, in the sense of the mathematical, physical, and biological sciences, has an object, which is the world of bodies, and in the hierarchy of reality the world of bodies is the lowest domain. Beyond it lies the jurisdiction of what is not merely the world of bodies but the world of persons, the world of the values of the spirit, subsisting in a personal manner. This world of persons is a concrete world, as real as, and more real than, the world of bodies, and finally more interesting, for in practice our relations with persons are more important than our relations with matter. All that concerns our relations with persons, the knowledge of others, personal love, friendship, communion between men, is infinitely more important than the material world. For myself I should even say that this alone seems absolutely real. In other words, I should admit that it is possible to question the reality of the external world—I don't question it myself, but this would, I grant, be possible. But I cannot possibly question the reality of the other, for he is something which resists me far more than matter, resists me not only in the sense of a material resistance against which I dash myself, but of a value which I cannot refuse to recognize. I simply cannot refuse to the other that essential respect which is love, I cannot make use of him like an instrument, I cannot refuse him the right to existence. To do so would be contradictory to what I recognize myself to be: a person who has the right to freedom, respect, and love.

Consequently there is nothing more objective than persons, and it must be said that the real world is essentially the human world, for which the material world is in a way only the conditioning. When the Bible speaks of the resurrection of the body, it certainly does not mean that we shall recover the atoms of nitrogen which served—very provisionally, for a few hours of our life—to support our personal life; it means essentially that we shall rise again as personal beings, that is, as beings comprising all the concrete reality signified precisely by the word "body." It is this concrete character of the person, essentially signified by corporeity, which is the material support of the values of intelligence and love, and thus confers on them their concrete character.

It is therefore supremely important for us to be sure whether we can know one another and love one another. When Sartre, in *Huis-clos*, sees the "other" as that which resists him, and says: "Hell is other people" (that is, hell is the resistance offered by the reality of the other), he faces the problem. But he answers it wrongly, for this resistance of the other—inasmuch as it results, on the contrary, in my recognizing the other's right to exist alongside me, and in the relation thus established between us—is what constitutes human life as distinct from animal life. In this respect, everything which offers me this knowledge of the other, everything connected with what Pascal called the spirit of perception, *l'esprit de finesse,* everything connected with metaphysics, in the sense of being an assertion that mind surpasses matter and that there are things beyond physics, everything connected with the philosophy of testimony and speech, that is, with the modes of communication between me and others, everything connected with true speech and with trust in speech, everything connected with the possibility of a real exchange with the other, which is the condition of all genuine love:—all this introduces us to a sphere of both existence and knowledge which is as objective as strictly scientific knowledge, and far more important. For it is obvious that at this level the person of the other is not an object we can know by the methods of science, which can analyze only objects.

Now the "other" is never an object; he is always, to me, irreducible and impermeable in his essential being. I cannot take possession of the person of the other and dissect it, as I can a guinea pig, and if I think I can, I deceive myself. All the psychologists and psychoanalysts would be deluded if they thought they could exhaust the person of the other by scientific methods. What they reach is really never more than a periphery: real, but not penetrating the essential being. That can simply never be captured. It is a mystery, the mystery of the person. I can only have access to it when the other communicates it to me. This means that there is no access to the knowledge of the person except in the revelation which the person makes of himself to me, when he really wishes to communicate to me his inaccessible secret. I have already quoted the saying of Scheler: "Silence is the characteristic of persons." A rose expresses all that it is; it has nothing to tell me but what is expressed by its scent, its color, and its thorns. It has no other secret, it is wholly unveiled and therefore does not need to be revealed. Whereas the characteristic of the person is precisely that it is much more than is expressed by its outward reality. If I claimed to know it solely by its outward aspect, I should miss its secret, that secret which, the Bible says, even the angels do not penetrate. And so, if I wish to come to the knowledge of what matters supremely, that is, of what the other is, I can reach it only to the extent that the other is willing to communicate what he is. In other words, at this level love is the measure of knowledge.

We shall never be able to know that essence of the other's person except by the revealing word. I can only know the secret of a heart insofar as that heart is itself willing to express itself to me by speech. This means that when we reach this higher level of reality we have to do with a new mode of knowledge, a mode which is capable of a certainty equal, if not superior, to scientific knowledge. As we learn from Pascal, whose evidence is of eminent value, for he was eminent in all fields, the spirit of geometry has an object which is the world of bodies, but when one comes to the world of hearts we need another method, another process, which he calls the spirit of *finesse* (fine perception), but which is connected with just that penetration of the other through communication. It is good scientific method to apply to each object the method which is suitable for it. It is bad method to try to apply to the things of the heart a method which is valid only for the things of the body.

But if even at the human level we know the other only by revelation, that is, insofar as he reveals or unveils himself or gives himself to us, this will be eminently true of our relation with a personal God. The claim of the human mind to try to get possession of God as of an object, like something which is an object of science, on the same level as the phenomena of the material world, is an absurdity. It is obvious that we can never have access to a personal and living God by the same way as that which serves for knowledge of the objects of the material world. The only problem, then, is to know whether he has effectively revealed himself to us. That is why faith is adherence to a fact, to the actual reality of a manifestation of God, which proves to be that by which we can have access to him. It is precisely this which is the object of all Scripture. The whole of Scripture, Old and New Testaments alike, has no other object than to be a testimony to that event, that fact. Here we enter on another order of realities. Up to now we have been on the level of common and universal human experience; now we appeal to the fact of a revelation of the living God. It is most important to emphasize this, for it constitutes the radical difference between religion in general and revelation in particular.

THE HISTORY OF SALVATION

Now, what is the object of this revelation? What is the object of all Scripture? It is to tell us, not directly what God is, but what God does. The whole of Scripture is sacred history, that is, testimony to the intervention of God in history. The faith of the Jews and the Christians bears, not on the fact that God exists, but on the fact that God has intervened in the history of men. There are therefore two kinds of history; there is the history of the great works of men, of which the religions form part, for the religions are among the highest masterpieces of the human genius, along with his scientific, political, and aesthetic creations. For us, Greece is forever Archimedes and Phidias, but also Plato and Plotinus. In the Bible we find another kind of history, not the history of the creations of the human genius, but that of the interventions of God among mankind. The problem is, how far can we give our adherence to this *datum* of fact?

It is, then, through his works that God shows what he is, and this is the object of sacred history. Its object is to show us that in the web of human history, which is the history of art, of politics, of economy, there are some actions which are divine actions. That is to say that God breaks into the world of phenomena in the midst of which we live. The choice of Abraham in the Old Testament is not simply the development and evolution of the religious history of the Semitic world in the second millennary before Christ. This is an absolute beginning. Yahweh comes to find this man whom he has created, in order to create in him a new people. This idea of creation, in the sense of an absolute beginning, is one of the marks of the living God. God is he who creates, that is, who produces an absolute beginning. To take another example, the incarnation of the Word, which with the resurrection is the fundamental object of our faith, is essentially a creative action, in which the living God produces in Mary, by his own creative power, the manhood of Jesus. So, as I have already said, the mystery of the virginal conception, which is one of those which even many Christians find most incomprehensible and would willingly relegate to the realm of the marvelous or fantastic, is seen instead to be one of the most evident, inasmuch as it means that what begins in Jesus is a new mankind, and that the Word of God, who in the beginning had formed the first Adam from the earth of Paradise, as Scripture says (or in a quite different way, as we have a perfect right to believe), comes to seek that man in a daughter of his race in order to resume possession of him and lead him to that last end for which he was destined. That is why St. Paul tells us that Christ is the beginning of a new mankind, and that the resurrection of the manhood of Jesus is an event comparable to the original creation of the world and of man. This is then to testify by the very fact to the existence of divine actions. Sacred history is the history of the great things that God performs. To this fact we must constantly return, for it is the very object of faith. A Christian is not merely one who believes that God exists. All the pagans believe that God exists. But it is necessary to be a Christian in order to believe that God has intervened in history.

God creates, produces from nothing; God makes his covenant, that is, he communicates his own gifts; God dwells in the midst of his people, and in Jesus Christ he dwells in the midst of his Church. And according to the words: "If anyone love me, we shall come to him and make our abode with him," there is an indwelling of the Trinity in the Christian heart. God saves, that is, he can rescue us from any situation, however desperate, and from spiritual misery and the misery of death. These are all things which man cannot do, which absolutely exceed his capacity, and Scripture tells us, not only that God can do them, but that God has done them; so that a Christian is one who knows that he is re-created in Christ, who knows that he is saved from evil and from death, that he is the abode of the Trinity, that he has entered into the covenant, which is Christ, and that he is already justified: "He who believes in me has been judged already." And that is precisely what constitutes the essential object of faith, that it is not a matter of possibilities but of realities already obtained.

The Christian is one for whom the essential is already obtained. For in Jesus Christ the essential is already obtained. Nothing as important as the resurrection will ever happen again. Man's destiny is already decided in substance. That is what faith is. We do not just hope that things will work out; we know that mankind is already, in substance, saved, and that it is up to every man to appropriate that salvation by faith. That causes St. Paul to say that we are heirs, that is, that we already possess in substance, in faith, the spiritual gifts, and are simply waiting to enter into the full enjoyment of what we already possess in substance. A Christian is therefore one for whom there is no doubt as to the final issue, neither for the life of mankind nor for his personal life, insofar as he believes that in Christ all this is already achieved. He only waits patiently for the day when he will enter into possession of that which is already obtained for him in Christ.

It is important to repeat these things, for that is precisely what faith is, and many Christians nowadays are confused on this question of faith. It must first be explained what it is about, what we hold and why we hold it. These are the two problems: in what do I believe, and why do I believe in it? We must be able to reply to these questions, in dialogue with any of our contemporaries. Well, what I believe in is that God has intervened in the history of man, that the gulf which man could not cross has been crossed by God, that God has come toward me to find me and make me a sharer in his own life. That is the sum total of faith. It is to believe that this has already happened, and through this manifestation of God it is then revealed what God is. The knowledge of God given me by the Old and New Testaments does not consist of a discourse about God. It is not at all a treatise of theology.

Theology, the theologians, would produce that later, as they had to do (I shall explain why, later). But the Bible, sometimes to our disappointment, is not a theological treatise. It is essentially a history. It tells of things that happened. It tells us how God acted in the beginnings of the human race, it tells us the story of Abraham, of Noah, of Elijah, the story of Jesus Christ, and then the story of the apostles.

This is the root difference between the Bible of the Christians and the books of all the other religions. The books of the religions are theologies or mythologies, that is, speculations about God. The book of the Christians is a history, a very historical history, which is unfolded in the web of the history of the Near East, and yet a history with this difference from the history of Herodotus or the history of Livy, that it is not simply the history of the great things done by the Jewish people, as Herodotus tells of the great things done by the Athenians, or Livy tells of the great things done by the Romans. On the contrary, the sacred history is rather damaging for the people of Israel; it is not in the least triumphalist; there is nothing less triumphalist than the Old Testament. The Old Testament is a damaging indictment; it is practically the history of Israel's sins. But on the other hand, if the Old Testament is a damning indictment for the people of Israel, it is the story of the great things Yahweh has done in Israel. What matters in the Old Testament, as in the New, is not what men do, but what God does. The history of Israel and the history of the Church are written to the glory of God, that is, they show forth not the greatness of man but the greatness of God, not the triumphs of the genius of man but the greatness of what God can bring about in the hearts of men who are, nonetheless, miserable sinners. And there we find ourselves in the presence of something absolutely different.

It is this fact which has enabled a great contemporary historian, Butterfield, to say that the Bible is ultimately the only way to attain historical objectivity, for otherwise, he says, it is very difficult for a history to avoid being an apologia, difficult for historians to avoid defending a thesis. Burkhardt defends the thesis of the influence of the genius of great men. The Marxists maintain that history is explained by the class war and the gradual emancipation of the proletariat. Others explain history as a succession of civilizations governed by a sort of biological rhythm. On the contrary, Butterfield says, the only key to history is that of universal sin, and the only way to historical objectivity is to renounce self-justification; as long as one tries to justify oneself, objectivity is impossible. Any history which is a defense or an apologia is in the end a history which falsifies facts. Whereas to defend any human cause is precisely what Isaiah and the prophets do not attempt; they defend only one cause, the cause of God.

It is through these ways in which God acts that, as we read the Bible, we familiarize ourselves with the ways of the living God. We can say that the reading of Scripture is just that. It familiarizes us with the ways of action of the living God, ways of action which *a priori* are disconcerting, which do not correspond with our logic, but their reality is impressed on us all through that wonderful continuity of the Old Testament, the New Testament, and the Church. For God always acts in the same way. We can authenticate the divine ways; they are different from men's ways of action. It is a fact that the same ways of action are met in the Old Testament, when Yahweh saves his people from Egypt, as are met in the New Testament, when God delivers the manhood of Jesus out of death, and are met in the sacraments, when the power of divine grace delivers the catechumen from the captivity in which he was bound. It is this fact which bears in itself, ultimately, a sort of evidence, by facing us with a certain order of things whose reality, through their very continuity, forces itself on us. It seems impossible that this continuity of four thousand years, in which we always see the same ways of action on God's part, should not correspond to something real. This means, then, that the way of access to the knowledge of God in the Old Testament will be meditation on sacred history. Its point of departure is therefore quite different from religious knowledge, which was meditation on nature. We can say that we pass from nature to history, and that the mark of the biblical revelation is precisely to be a manifestation of God through the history of God's people.

SCRIPTURE

But, as I said just now, there is also another problem to be faced, not *what* I believe, but *why*. On the former, I said: God has intervened in the history of man. But what is the ground of my right to believe this impossible fact, that God has intervened in the history of man? What justifies my right to hold to the truth of the sacred history? What justifies my right to believe that in Abraham Yahweh intervened in history to raise up a people for himself? What justifies my right to believe that Jesus was born by the power of the Spirit and not by the ordinary laws of human generation? What justifies my right to believe that this flesh of mine, assumed by Christ, is now already, by his ascension, plunged into the abyss of God? If these actions are divine, the authority on which I rely in order to believe in them, must also be something divine, something in which I must be able to place absolute trust. Have I the right to place absolute trust in the testimony of Scripture?

Revelation in fact means two things, that God acts, and that God speaks. In other words, when I speak of faith, I am concerned with two things. Ultimately, the goal of faith is events, not speeches. To believe is not, in the first place, to believe in dogmas, but to believe in events, and essentially in the resurrection of Christ. But it is also to believe in the word through which that event was communicated to me, for I have no access to it directly. The resurrection of Christ is not something which I can verify experimentally. I have access to it only through the testimony which affirms it. Here, then, we meet this aspect of revelation at a second stage. Have I the right to believe in the word which tells me these improbable things?

This is the Christian's situation, and it must be fully accepted. Until we have got down to this root, our faith is still more or less affective or sentimental, but not fully grounded. Have I the right to commit the whole of my intellect to the resurrection of Christ, in the face of any of my contemporaries, of a Marxist, of a Moslem, of a Jew, of a Hindu, of any man whatever, in full certainty and full clarity? That is the question put to each of us, the question we have to answer. Most of us have received the faith through a social or family tradition, but we have got to accept it fully, for only so can we testify to it, not as a wager, not as a hope, but as a certainty on which we stake all. For a Christian is one who stakes all on his faith. Faith completely transforms the very idea of existence.

It is clear that if Jesus is risen, if we are called to rise with him, if that is the final meaning of life, my vision of what happens in the world is now entirely transformed. The tragedy of Christianity today is just that so many Christians are weak in faith. Fifty years ago Péguy said that the great sickness of the Christian world was its profound lack of charity; today I should say that it was its profound lack of faith. We are sensitive to the call of charity; not that we are ever altogether faithful to it, no one ever is; but we are sensitive to the call of charity, that is, to material and spiritual sufferings. We understand that it is impossible to be a Christian without charity, but we sometimes think it possible to be a Christian without faith.

There are many today who imagine that one can be a Christian when one practices charity, but that it is not necessary to have faith. In other words, that Christianity consists essentially in the love of our neighbor, not essentially in faith in the resurrection of Christ. The dissociation of these two aspects is always destructive. For if the Christian who has faith without love is a scandal, the Christian who has love without faith is equally a scandal. His testimony is destructive. Instead of truly building in Christ, he gives others the impression that to be a Christian it suffices to perform certain duties to others. But this is unfaithful to Christ. To be faithful to Christ one must be faithful to the wholeness of Christ. Now the wholeness of Christ implies love of our brethren, but also faith in the word of God, which is the only foundation of genuine charity. No illusion needs to be more vigorously denounced than that of those who claim to give charity, or love of our neighbor, a sort of self-sufficiency, enabling us to dispense with faith in God.

In the last resort everything depends on this. The problem is, then, to know whether we have the right to believe in those divine actions, and so to know on what grounds we believe in them. Now Scripture tells us not only that these actions took place, but that the way by which we have access to them is also a divine action. It is what we call the inspiration of Scripture, the fact that the scriptural authors state that what they tell us, they tell us in the name, not only of a human authority, but of a divine authority. It is by the power and light of God himself that they tell us what they do. On the inspiration of Scripture, Jews, Protestants, Catholics, and Orthodox all agree. Scripture is not a human story of divine things; Scripture itself is divine speech, that is, the writers of Scripture wrote it under the inspiration of the Holy Spirit. We put our trust not merely in some very intelligent, very honest men, but in the word of God. God is he in whom we believe, but God is also he through whom we believe.

To believe means both to believe God and to believe in God. I mean that to believe is to trust the word of God. It is on the word of God that I believe in the actions of God: it is on God that I rely. And so my faith can be indestructible once for all, for it is founded, as the Old Testament says, on the rock, on a testimony which cannot possibly deceive me.

I have access to the heart of one I love through his or her words. It is only by words that I can communicate with the other. A world in which there is no trust in the other's word is a world in which nothing is any longer possible. A world in which I no longer trust anyone is ultimately a world of utter solitude, the world of despair. Those who are incapable of trusting shut themselves up in the world of despair, because what is finally essential in life is the relation with the other, and that always implies a certain trust, and this is a fundamental and legitimate human need. There are persons whom we have the right to trust. Trust is not something which is always inevitably betrayed, as a certain inhuman pessimism of today would have us believe.

Our relations with God are of this sort. They are essentially grounded, here too, on the word. The problem is to know whether I can trust God, whether I have the right and therefore the duty to trust that word when that word is addressed to me. At this point I must examine the Scriptures, to see if I have the right to see in them the word of God. But when I observe in them that continuity of truth, when on the other hand I observe that those who attest that truth are witnesses who deserve that I should believe them, when finally the supreme witness is Christ himself, engaging all his authority in affirming that in him the word of God speaks to me, then I touch something so fundamental that I know I have the right to trust him absolutely.

In other words, there are ultimately only two alternatives in our human situation. Either I have the right to trust Jesus Christ, the right to have faith, or I have not the right to trust him, and then I have no right to trust anyone. For if Christ is a false witness, there is no true witness. If Christ deceives me, there is nobody whom I can trust. If the word of Christ is not a word of truth, if in Jesus Christ (whom every man recognizes as at least the moral and religious apex of mankind), I am faced with falsehood (or with what is as despicable as falsehood: illuminism, something which has no consistency), then finally, I must say it, the world has no meaning; it is the absurd which is right and in the end despair is the only answer to existence. That is the choice with which we are confronted: either the word of Christ, or despair. That means that if the word of Christ is a lying word, there is no other escape, nothing has meaning.

Therefore it is a question of knowing, not simply whether God has intervened, but whether we have the right to believe that he has intervened. That God should have been able to take part in our history is, on the face of it, improbable and incredible. Faith is a contradiction of the probable in the name of the true. It is the property of faith not to rely on the probable, on what is natural. What is natural is that God should keep to his domain and man to his. What is paradoxical is that God should be in man's domain, and that man should be in God's. All Christianity is summed up in this, that God came to seek man and that man can go to God. All is summed up in two things, to know whether Jesus is God, that is, whether God has really come down to the sphere of human life, and second, to know whether man is divinized, that is, whether our humanity is called to share the life of God. Here there are essentially two paradoxical statements. On the one hand, that God came down into the world of man, which is what we call love—"he loved me and gave himself for me"—and second, that man, upheld by the power of the deity, is raised above nature and introduced to the sphere of the divine life, in a blessed and incorruptible existence. It is the affirmation of the resurrection, which we believe to have been accomplished in Jesus Christ, and which, once accomplished in Jesus Christ, we are called to share. The whole mystery of the Son is summed up in the two essential mysteries: the Incarnation and the Resurrection. The Incarnation is the staggering event of God's coming down to man. The Resurrection is the staggering event of man rising up to God.

At this point arises the problem: have we the right to believe such astonishing things? On what authority do we believe them? Now this is the second aspect of the problem of faith, which is not only belief in the event but belief also in the word. I mean, belief that the text which tells us of these events is one which we have the right to trust. It is the problem of Scripture. But the problem of Scripture is raised in relation to the problem of Sacred History [because Scripture is simply a testimony to Sacred History]. Have we the right to believe in that testimony? It is one thing to know that an event happened, another thing to believe in the testimony of him who reports it. The problem of Scripture is not the problem of the history; it is secondary in relation to the problem of the history. But it is through Scripture that we reach the history, and it is essential to know whether we have the right to believe in the testimonies which tell us of these events. Now the Christian affirmation is that we have the right to believe in these testimonies, because we believe these divine things on a divine testimony. Not only is the history Sacred History, but the scripture is also Sacred Scripture. It rests not only on the authority of the men who wrote it, but on the help of the Holy Spirit.

That is to say, and this is vital, that what matters in the Bible is not nearly so much the evidence for the known object as the veracity of the witness. The ground for the adherence of our intellect is not so much that we have the evidence for the thing as that he who testifies to it deserves to be completely trusted. This mode of knowledge is not an

inferior mode; on the contrary, it is a mode of knowledge
which corresponds to the higher realities, and it is a way of
access to certitude as valid as that of evidence, precisely for
those things which are not susceptible of evidence, just because of their value. Let me explain: we can have evidence
of something, we can gain possession of it by our intellect,
only if it is something below our intellect, that is, if it belongs
to the material world and can be the object of scientific
knowledge. But as I have already said, as soon as we rise to
the level of persons, no scientific knowledge can enable us
to penetrate the inner life of another's person. We can only
know the other's person insofar as he reveals himself to us.
That means that at this point the only question is whether
we can trust that person. Thus the most important certitudes
of life, the vital certitudes, those which concern all human
relations, such as the oath and the promise, are essentially
bound up with the quality of the trust we can give to the
person's word. What is so serious nowadays is that, because
of the way in which the word has so often been abused, so
many minds are unable to trust the word. This spoils communication between persons, because that communication is
based on the word, and its rule is that the word can be trusted.
To the Jews there was no graver sin than false witness, because they had that profound sense of the importance of
the word.

This is of vital importance, because what troubles so many
men today about faith is the act of adhering to something for
which they have not the evidence. Now, this means that they
apply the methods which belong to the criticism of scientific knowledge to matters which pertain essentially to the
criticism of testimony, and this is a fundamental error of
method. The first mark of a scientific method is to apply to
each object the method which is appropriate for it. That is
the beginning of science. Anyone who tried to apply the
methods of geometry to the problem of God would be com-

pletely at sea, because this involves another method. For the things of the body, geometry; for the things of the soul, perception (*finesse*); for the things of God, prophecy, that is, the word. We cannot know the deep things of God except insofar as God makes them known to us. This means that faith, so far from being an inferior form of certitude, is the supreme form. It is that very form which corresponds to the highest objects. In other words, it is absurd to suppose that we can have access to God otherwise than by faith; it is absurd to imagine that God is an object which can be mastered as a material object is mastered. If God is essentially a personal being, we can only know that personal being insofar as he reveals himself to us. So the whole problem concerns the testimony through which God reveals himself.

To have faith, then, is to believe that Jesus Christ is so dependable that I can rely on him utterly; it is to place full reliance on Christ and, fully relying on him, to believe what he says and to hope for what he promises. Relying, then, on Jesus Christ, I believe in the resurrection of the body, I believe in eternal life, I believe in the communion of saints. And why do I believe all this? Not because I have the evidence for it, but because I can rely with my whole self on Jesus Christ who tells it to me.

CHAPTER VII

THE HOLY TRINITY

We come now to the specifically Christian revelation of God, the mystery of the Trinity. We have first to establish the basis of this revelation in the New Testament. The Trinity is revealed to us from the viewpoint of the history of salvation, that is, of the actions of the Trinity in the world. Here we meet what is the most elementary and at the same time the most mysterious truth in Christianity. The most elementary, inasmuch as the specific mark of Christianity is essentially the revelation of the Trinity. It is the very object of baptism: "I baptize thee in the name of the Father and of the Son and of the Holy Ghost." It is the very substance of the Mass, in which we offer to the Father the priestly action of the incarnate Son, in the unity of the Holy Spirit. The whole of Christianity is there. Not to put the Trinity at the heart of Christianity would be to miss its essence altogether.

It is also the greatest mystery, for the Trinity is an unfathomable abyss. At the same time, if we perceive its ultimate significance, this mysterious reality throws a marvelous light on the most ordinary daily life. So far from it being an abstraction which does not concern us in our life, it is certain that nothing concerns us more in our daily life than the Trinity. For to affirm the Trinity is to affirm that in God there are three persons; and to affirm that the "Three" is as primordial as the "One" signifies something pregnant with meaning, namely, that love is coeval with being, that is, that the absolute is not an impersonal unity in which everything is finally destined to be dissolved, but a trinity of persons in a communion of love. Now this revolutionizes everything, for if the ground of the absolute is love, communion between persons will also be a reflection of the absolute in creation. Here we find the basis of what we know by experience to be supremely real, the two final assertions which we know we can never refuse to accept: the dignity of the person of the other, and the imperative of love.

THE BIBLICAL DATA

If we ask ourselves what is, after all, the object of our belief, it is this: "We know and believe the love God has for us." The love we believe in is not simply that between persons, for that would make no difference between a Christian and any other. We believe that the ground of the love between persons is the existence of love in God. This gives the Christian vision an extraordinary unity. What makes the commandment of love the supreme commandment in our relations with others is the fact that love is really what constitutes the absolute itself. It is essential to state this at the outset, in order to show how intimately the mystery of the Trinity concerns us. When, in the last resort, we have to find the basis of the fundamental attitudes of our life, it is to this that we have to return. But this, which is the object of our faith, being stated, how do we arrive at it, how do we know that God is three, how do we know that in God there is this mysterious Trinity?

The foundation of this has first to be established. (Here I am trying, above all, to lay the foundations.) For the problem today is the foundation of faith. It is essential that the objects of our faith should be seen to be so grounded that we can feel we have a right to hold them in the fullness of a perfectly lucid, perfectly critical, perfectly free intelligence. There can be no question of attaching ourselves to what we regard as merely a heritage, a tradition, or the expression of an attraction. It is a question of something which we have the right to affirm before any non-believer today, as being the truth, and not simply a personal position. The problem is that of truth. Otherwise there can be no pertinent discussion, no dialogue possible, where one does not believe in the truth. We believe that a truth exists. We believe that that truth is the Trinity. But this is a vast assertion, enormous, paradoxical. When we make it to an atheist today his first reaction is naturally to say: "By what right do you claim to say that I must believe in the Trinity?" Now that is precisely what I hold. I hold that I have a right to require any atheist of today, not only to believe in man, not only to believe in God, but to believe in the Trinity, because the Trinity is the truth. And that is what believing is: to believe that this is the real, not a hypothesis about the real. Hypotheses matter little: what matters is to know what is the real.

Now the Christian affirmation is that the fundamental thing is the Trinity. The Trinity is the absolute itself, the abyss of being, the ultimate foundation, which is revealed to man in Jesus Christ, so that when the blindness of our present existence is removed, all without exception, Mohammed, Confucius, Karl Marx, whoever you will, all will finally be confronted with the Trinity. That is why the apostleship exists, because it is charitable to warn people in advance. The condition of any sincere dialogue with a non-Christian is to begin by saying: "I must warn you that one day you will be confronted with the Trinity." After that, we can talk about syndical action, international cooperation or any problem we like, but first we must warn him that one day he will be confronted with the Trinity. That is what it means to believe: to believe that there is a truth, and that truth is the Trinity. But we undertake a hard task when we say that this is an established fact, that we claim to present it, not as an arbitrary hypothesis, but as grounded in the very reality of the facts. This is what must be tackled, for it is so important that no ambiguity about it can be allowed.

We must always come back to what is elementary. What I am trying to do in this book is to get back to the essential bases of the faith, for I think that what so many Christians lack today is assured grounds for their faith, and that we must never weary of returning to those grounds. Only thus can the Christian bear witness to the truth, that is, to the one and only vocation of all men. It is no use putting forward a particular opinion in the vast concert of opinions, which would only lead in the end to making Christianity a subjective preference. We have got to establish the truth of Christianity. The only question is whether we have the right to say that Christianity is the truth, the real; whether finally the real is not the nuclear composition of matter, but the Trinity. For my part, I believe that the reality is not matter: I know that the basis of reality is the Trinity. By reality we mean that which cannot be questioned. Those who question it are deceived. The problem is how to have access to the real. Nothing matters but the real. The problem is how to know that which is, to know what we are and what we shall be. Now, our affirmation is that the Trinity is the basis of the real, and that the Trinity can be reached by man, through the revelation given us in Jesus Christ. It is Jesus Christ who introduces us to reality.

The starting point is Scripture. But the object of faith is beyond Scripture, for faith is not directed to a Scripture but to a reality which is known through Scripture. That is to say that the goal of the intellect is never the concept for its own sake, but the reality which is grasped through the concept. The concept is no great matter; what matters to me is the reality I grasp. It is the same here; the Scripture is only an instrument. I do not believe in the Scripture, I believe in what Scripture makes known to me. And what is that? Scripture makes known to me three *data* (*données*)—I purposely use this word because of its note of indetermination—and on these *data* I shall then have to reflect. I shall end by saying that these *data* are persons. But historically these *data* were not called persons till the fourth century. There is no mention of the three persons in any passage of the New Testament, but there is mention of the Father, of the Son, of the Holy Spirit. And these are what I call the three *data*. So what is primitive (in the New Testament) and what compels acceptance is that there is, first, the Father, next, that there is the Son—Christ—and then that there is the Spirit.

It was then the task of theological elaboration to say what these *data* are. What was primary was the reality, that the Christians found themselves confronted with something real, something resistant, something which imposed itself, which was there, which could not be manipulated at will. There was tentative discussion on these three *data,* in which men began by saying things about them which were inaccurate. It was like when you make a portrait of someone and the first sketch doesn't satisfy you. You rub it out and try again. And so it was from one approximation to another that the formulas adequate to the fact (*donné*) were found. And these formulas were difficult to find, for this fact was in no way preconditioned, it had no earlier equivalent, it was an absolute novelty. Formulating the fact correctly is what we call theology. Theology always begins with inaccurate language. In this sense, historically, heresy always comes before orthodoxy; the heretic is the man who persists in abandoned positions, when a correct position—or at least more correct, less incorrect—has been proposed.

We must never, then, confuse the formula with the fact. And when I say that there are three persons in God, this is a formula which dates from the fourth century. It was then that in the east men began to speak of *tria prosopa. Prosopon* in Greek means "mask." The Latin equivalent is *persona,* which perhaps means "mask," that is, practically "voice-carrier," that *through* which the sound, *sonus,* passes—unless it comes from the Etruscan *phersûn,* the proper name of a person who can be seen in one of the burial grounds of the Tarquinia. But in any case men started from expressions which meant the "mask," the mask signifying the "personage," in the sense of the "characters" in a play, and the "personage" finally served to denote the person. That is the etymological development of the word. From that time men began to speak of the three persons, as being the formula which seemed most adequate to express that irreducible fact, which is offered us by the reality of which we speak.

THE PRESENCE OF GOD

What then is the fact behind these formulations? It is first of all the Father, the First Person, he whom the early Christians called God, *ho Theos.* It is very striking to see that the expression *ho Theos* is reserved to the Father by Scripture and the first theologians. He is the God to whom the whole Old Testament testifies, and who appears there with all those characteristics we have seen in our study of the Old Testament. Throughout the Old Testament revelation there is a reality which forces itself on us with its qualities of sovereign existence, existential intensity, and overwhelming greatness, all displayed in an absolutely awesome sanctity and culminating in a supremely desirable beauty. The progress of the knowledge of God in the Old Testament advances from holy fear to ecstatic adoration, from the point where God appears in his aspect of utter separation from us to the point where he is seen to call forth from us a homage of total devotion. I need not repeat this, which is the content of the entire Old Testament, the experience of Abraham, of Moses, of Isaiah; it is what Jews, Moslems, and Christians acknowledge in common when they confess the existence of a transcendent

God, an existence which absolutely compels their acceptance. I need not repeat here how that reality makes itself felt in us. I recall only that we encounter the sacred when we recognize, in the innermost center of our own lives, things which we realize are quite inescapable. They compel our acceptance in spite of ourselves, not in virtue of any external constraint but of an inner demand which we cannot refuse.

In this fundamental human experience I meet someone in me who is more myself than I am; in myself and in my experience I touch something which does not proceed from myself, but which forces itself on me. It is that experience which is rejected by atheism, in the Marxist or Sartrean sense of the word, which regards my freedom as that which constitutes both morality and metaphysics. But this contradicts real human experience. I know that I am not the one who lays down what is good or evil, true or false, but one who is confronted with a fact which forces itself on me, and to which I cannot deny myself.

This fact is God, in his aspect of fatherhood. The title of Father can be applied to God at three different levels. It can be applied to him in the sense of a universal fatherhood. Plato called God "father of the universe." This means that God is the source and therefore the father of the universe, and that this universe is the work of his love. In the New Testament Christ says: "Be sons of your Father who is in heaven, for he . . . sends rain on the just and on the unjust." There is a universal fatherhood of God, which is accessible to all men and concerns all men; God gives the blessings of nature to all men. This coincides with what I have earlier called the cosmic revelation, that is, the universal relation of God to all men through the blessings of nature.

There is a second sense, in which God is called Father by the Jewish people. Here fatherhood signifies the special relation between Israel and Yahweh. That special relation is expressed in the Old Testament by various metaphors taken from family relationships. God is called impartially father of the people of Israel, or mother of the people of Israel—"As a mother pities her children, so have I pitied you"—or the husband of the people of Israel. The different expressions are all equivalent and all denote the Covenant.

But there is a third sense in which God is Father, in an absolutely unique sense: that in which he is the Father of the only Son. Fatherhood in God now means something exclusive, the eternal relation of the Father with the Son, which embodies the fact that the Father eternally expresses himself in that perfect image of himself which is the Son. In this sense the only Son alone is Son, Christ alone is Son of the Father in the strict sense. Now, the content of the Christian revelation is that we are called, by becoming one with the only Son, to become children of the Father in the sense in which the only Son is Son of the Father. Here it is a case, not simply of that sonship which belongs to every man as creature, nor of that sonship which belongs to Israel as the people of the Covenant, but of a share in the unique sonship which belongs to the Son. That is why all Christianity consists in saying that we are called to share the privileges of the Son of God, and ourselves to become sons in the sense in which Christ is Son, so that with Christ and in Christ we should all be children of the Father.

I need not say how very elementary this is in Christianity. If we take the prayers of the Mass, we find that they are all addressed to God "through our Lord Jesus Christ thy Son, in the unity of the Holy Spirit." The prayers of the Mass are not addressed to an impersonal God, but to the Father, through the Son, in the Spirit. They express the fact that our prayer is the actual prayer of the Son, that prayer which is infallibly granted and in which we can speak to God with the freedom of the sons of God. That means that we are no longer in the state of fear and trembling, but in the freedom of the children of God, who are already, as St. Paul says, heirs of the divine blessings, which we already possess in substance, with the certainty that we shall possess them one day in fullness.

This touches one of the essential aspects of the Christian life, that man's attitude toward God is no longer that of servants, for, as Christ himself said, "I no longer call you servants but friends." The friend is the one to whom we entrust everything. We are brought into the Son, who possesses all the riches of the Father, so that we too may share in the riches of God. Once again, to the carnal man this is an incredible paradox, yet for the Christian it is the foundation of his faith. To be a Christian means to believe that this impossible thing is real. Fatherhood, in the sense understood by the New Testament, is therefore something quite different from a vague universal providence. It is the affirmation of the relationship between the Father and the only Son, and of our sharing in that relationship.

THE FACT OF CHRIST

At the level of the New Testament we meet a second fact: Jesus Christ. In the New Testament there is absolutely nothing but Christ, but there certainly is Christ. Now, what is Jesus Christ? What is the fact of Jesus Christ? Here I can only repeat in a few propositions what I developed in *Les Aspects du Christ*. On the one hand, it is scientifically certain that Jesus Christ is man. No serious scholar disputes that there was a man called Jesus who lived in Galilee. Not a single serious exegete, atheist, Jew, or Protestant, now disputes it. Many exegetes deny that Jesus is the son of God. That is a quite different question, to which we shall return. But I know of no one of any importance who denies that Jesus is a historical character, for the mass of converging evidence that we have about him is of the same kind as what we have about other historical characters, whose existence nobody questions. Nobody questions the existence of Buddha or of Socrates, but we have no *data* about either which are any more precise than those we have about Jesus, coming from both Christian and non-Christian sources.

But the fact is that for many men Jesus is merely one of the greatest religious figures of mankind, perhaps the greatest figure of all religious history. Now there is another certainty which is equally scientific—and I stress the "scientific," meaning that which is absolutely beyond question by any honest mind—and what I am going to state is equally a scientific certainty. That certainty is, speaking quite literally, that Jesus of Nazareth claimed divine authority and dignity. I am not saying that Jesus had the right to do so; that is a further question. He died precisely because men challenged that right. He was put to death for blasphemy, and that is the decisive proof, woven into the web of his story, that he claimed a divine dignity. He was put to death on the evidence of a witness who accused him of declaring himself the equal of the Temple. The Temple, to every Jew, is the place of God's presence. The high priest then tore his garments and said: "He has blasphemed, making himself the equal of God. How think you?" The Sanhedrin replied: "He is worthy of death." That was a lawful sentence, for the Jewish law makes it a capital offense to blaspheme, which means for a man to make himself God. In that judgment the Jewish law is right. I mean that for a man to make himself God is a monstrous sin. The Jews, like the Moslems and the Christians, are the champions of something fundamental when they absolutely deny that any man has the right to make himself God. Denunciation of all idolatry is the primordial truth, common to a Jew, a Moslem, and a Christian. Only God is God.

Now it is quite clear that Jesus did claim to be God. That is a historical certainty. Not in the first place by words, but in a far more important way, he never ceased—and here I weigh my every word—to behave in a way which implied that he claimed divine authority and dignity. The examples of this are very clear. He claimed the right to forgive sins, and when he forgave the sins of the paralytic man, the Pharisees said: "This man blasphemes; who can forgive sins but God alone?" And that is obvious. For an ordinary man to claim to forgive sins would be madness. Sin is a matter between God and man. So the Pharisees understood perfectly well that when Jesus said: "Your sins are forgiven," he was claiming a power that belonged to God alone. When Christ said: "The Son of man is Lord even of the sabbath," the Pharisees said: "This man blasphemes," and they were right, for the sabbath was established by God, therefore God alone is Lord of the sabbath.

I have often told the story, but I think it is so instructive that I shall repeat it once more, of the conversation I had with a rabbi, who once said to me: "Father, there is only one thing for which we blame Jesus, and that is that he laid hands on the Law, for the Law was established on Sinai by Yahweh, and only God can modify what God has established." I replied: "Monsieur Rabbi, nothing you could say would please me better, for it is certain that Jesus did modify the Law, and that in fact means, and can only mean, one thing; if, as you say and rightly say, God alone can modify what God has established, then Jesus Christ claimed to have an authority equal to that of him who had established the Law, that is, of Yahweh on Sinai." The Jews understood him perfectly, and still understand him perfectly, and this argument is as valid for a Jew of today as for the Jewish contemporaries of Christ.

It is therefore scientifically indisputable that Jesus of Nazareth claimed an authority, a dignity, and finally a nature which are those of God. He claimed thus to belong to the sphere of God by his conduct, but he also claimed it by his words. Many examples could be given. St. John's Gospel is full of just this theme. "I and the Father are one." "I came from the Father and am come into the world; again I am leaving the world and going to the Father." It is therefore certain, and here I weigh my words, that on all that I have said here, every honest historian can only agree, and that I have said nothing which could not be accepted by every mind.

I now come to the problem which Jesus presents to every man. Jesus claimed divine authority. This cannot be an imposture. An impostor can present himself as a divine person. There have been impostors in history, there have been many persons who have declared themselves to be God, and have tried to form a following of disciples, but this has never lasted long. Again, a man who calls himself God may be a visionary. I call an impostor one who is in bad faith, who knows that he is not what he claims to be, but plays the part in order to deceive. I call a visionary one who, on the borders of madness and generosity, confuses the domains of the human and the divine, in a field where confusion is one of the most painful phenomena, in which certain forms of nervous disease take mystical forms. It is here that we can see that genuine religion is sane, wise, grounded first of all on reality, having nothing to do with certain forms of fanaticism. There may be fanatics, but precisely in these cases there is something disturbing and suspect, not in the sphere of intention, but in the sphere of reality itself.

Now all men without exception—and I am still on the plane of undisputed statements—agree in recognizing that Jesus is at least one of the greatest figures in human history. Read the books on Jesus written by Jews like Edmond Fleg, Robert Aron, Jules Isaac, Scholom Asch. They do not believe that Jesus is God, but they see him as one of the preeminent expressions of the race of Israel. Take the Moslems: Jesus, Isa, holds a considerable place in the Koran, and Mohammed saw him as the greatest of the prophets. Take the Hindus: Gandhi and Arabindo both held the Sermon on the Mount to be the highest peak of human religion. And the majority of atheists, whether a socialist like Barbusse, an existentialist like Jeanson, or a Marxist like Garaudy, recognize in Jesus, on the human level, a greatness to which they pay homage. None of them would ever say that Jesus is either an impostor or a visionary. They believe that he is not God, they think that he was the prisoner of a world-view prior to dialectical materialism, in which God had not yet been shown to be the "opium of the people." As Jesus did not know that religion is the opium of the people, he is therefore to be excused for believing in God and believing that he was God. So it is possible for a Marxist to respect Jesus, even in his religious character, insofar as a historical view allows him to hold that it was impossible for a man of that era to be otherwise. The opinion of the Marxists is that if Jesus had lived today, after the development of dialectical materialism, he would doubtless have recognized that religion is the opium of the people, just insofar as he was a highly intelligent man.

Now we come to the real problem, and it is this. First, it is indisputable that Jesus claimed a divine dignity. Second, it is indisputable that Jesus was neither an impostor nor a visionary. The problem then arises—this is the least I can say and I shall say no more, for up to now I have used no formula which cannot be accepted by any man, no formula which presupposes or implies the Christian faith—the problem arises, whether the credentials of Jesus Christ are not such that, although what he says is improbable and must *prima facie* be considered improbable (for it is absolutely improbable for a man to be God), his word should nonetheless be trusted, so that in this unique case the improbable should be the true, and that the accusation of blasphemy, laid by the Jews against Jesus, which in all other cases would have been a just judgment, should in this one case be found to fall to the ground.

Christians of all denominations are simply those who, having examined the credentials of Jesus, after a lucid, honest, and strict examination, ranging from textual criticism to the content of the affirmations, and bearing on the person of Jesus and the persons of his apostles (a process which of course not every Christian can undertake for himself, but which every Christian must know to have been undertaken today by thousands of exegetes who are serious scholars), Christians are those who, having examined all this, hold that they have the right and therefore the duty, in all intellectual honesty, as men of today, to recognize as true the fact that Jesus of Nazareth, who was a man living on earth, is at the same time the presence of God among men. But he is the God who speaks to God, God who addresses the Father, God who tells us: "I come from the Father and I go to the Father," God who is a person subsisting in himself, distinct from another person, who is, precisely, the person of the Father, the God whom he addresses.

Now this is what the New Testament lays upon us. This is the brute fact of which we speak. I sum it up in two formulas. The New Testament faces us, first, with the fact that Jesus is God, and, second, with the fact that Jesus is distinct from God; that is, distinct from the Father; God-sent, distinct from God who sends. This is the only affirmation which does justice to what the Scriptures say about Jesus, that he is a divine person. This preserves his mystery. But the precise quality of the mystery is that it forces itself on me, not in virtue of some logical deduction or of some inner need but, on the contrary, as a reality which upsets my intellectual habits and disturbs me in my demands of logic or of thought, yet forces itself on me as supremely real. For the real is that which forces itself on me in such a way that I cannot exclude it, however much I may want to. If what I have just said forced itself on me in virtue of an inner need in which this was already contained, I could always say that I had invented it. That is why (though I do not deny that there is a sense in which it is valid) I do not greatly care for that argument for the existence of God which consists in saying: "I have an infinite desire for happiness; no creature can satisfy that infinite desire for happiness, therefore there exists a being who can satisfy that infinite desire for happiness." I greatly distrust it. It is too simple. It is too like saying that God is the projection outside myself of a certain fundamental dissatisfaction. But after all, why should I not be one who is fundamentally dissatisfied? That is what Sartre would answer, and he would be right. Sartre is perfectly right when he says: "I bear in myself more than any object can give me." My freedom transcends all that the world can offer me. But is it necessary that I should be happy?

But that is precisely what Jesus Christ is not. Jesus Christ does not come to suit the demands of my intellect. He is very upsetting to the habits of my intellect. That is just why I have such difficulty in believing in him. He is still more upsetting to the smooth organization of my life. I should be much more at ease if Jesus Christ did not exist. That is why one of the atheists' arguments is radically false, the argument which represents Christianity as something consoling. It's easy to see they don't live inside it! The various humanisms can offer homes or lairs which are far more comfortable, far better cushioned, in which one can very calmly live one's very calm little life. If Jesus is certainly something, it is just that it is he who brings into our life, as Jacques Rivière said, immense upheavals. When there is love in our life, as we well know, we can never again be wholly our own. It is this hard fact, then, which the reasoning of the theologians gradually came, not to explain—for all this can never be matter for explanation—but to express correctly, by saying that the Son is a person, equal to the Father. But this formula has meaning only when confronted with the fact, the implications of which it expresses.

THE EXPERIENCE OF THE SPIRIT

The third Person appears to us first as a dimension of our existence, that is, as what may be called the spiritual. The third Person is "the Spirit," *Spiritus*. A dimension of our existence, first in the collective sense of the word, that is, of the Church. The Church is essentially the field of action of the Spirit. The Church displays a nature which cannot be reduced to comparison with other societies, inasmuch as the actions performed in the Church are real, but absolutely different from those performed in other societies. To take an example, in the university one passes examinations, one becomes a lecturer or a research worker, one hands on knowledge. There we are in one kind of order.

We know ourselves that the Church corresponds in our lives to another order of experience. As Péguy has said, there is what the schoolmaster says, and there is what the priest says—sometimes the opposite! But this corresponds to those sources which we recognize as genuine sources of knowledge and experience. We recognize the authenticity of what is taught us by our good teachers in the university, and we try to take it in and be faithful to it. But we also recognize the authenticity of what is said by our good teachers the priests, insofar as they too hand on to us a certain order of teaching, which is another order, but presents its own evidence. So we recognize that here is an order of knowledge and an order of life which are different from the order of our intellectual life, our emotional life, or our aesthetic life, and that is precisely what we call the spiritual life. The spiritual life is not that inner life which is common to Buddhists, Socratists, Christians, and others; it is life which is operated by the Spirit. That is, it is what God alone can operate in us when he converts our hearts, when he gives us hearts of flesh in place of hearts of stone, when he makes us love what our flesh hates:

humility, poverty, the service of others, when he brings us into an order of realities unattainable by our reason, but which is as convincing to us as the order attained by our reason, and perhaps more so. This is the order to which the Spirit leads us when he gives us the science of Christ, the science of the saints, of Paul, of Augustine, of John of the Cross, of the Curé of Ars and Thérèse of Lisieux. There we recognize an order of reality which is absolutely genuine. But it is not flesh and blood which has taught it to us, it is the Holy Spirit. It is the order of the saints, the order of holiness, the order of charity. It is a supremely real order, as those know who live in it. Through it they touch a reality of which they are in no way the source, for they are perfectly aware that it does not proceed from them. Therefore, as St. Paul says, they testify that "it is the Spirit himself bearing witness with our spirit that we are children of God" (Rom. 8. 16). It is that inner witness of the Holy Spirit that we know.

Here I return to my fundamental criterion: we know the Holy Spirit through what he does. I ask only the evidence of facts. But I challenge any atheist to give me an adequate explanation of St. Paul, of St. Augustine, of St. Thérèse of Lisieux, or the Curé of Ars. If I am ever given such an explanation, I shall admit that this is not an absolutely irreducible order. I have never yet come across any which was even a rough attempt at an explanation. The attempts at explanation which they offer are so absurd that they themselves do not dare present them to a Christian. For when they would reduce St. Thérèse to a sublimation of *eros,* when they would reduce St. Paul to a tension of the class war, they say things which are totally inadequate to their object, and thus have no adverse effect at all on the existence of a certain order of realities which are part and parcel of life and of history. I ask nothing more than the actual testimony of history, nothing but what all are obliged to allow me, and on the basis of that evidence I claim that I have the right to say: "This is not the work of man but of the Spirit of God, and of the Spirit of God alone."

"The spiritual," in the Christian sense, is what man performs in virtue, not of his natural capacities, but of what the gift of the Spirit, given to him, enables him to perform, beyond all natural strength. The Spirit is that which introduces us to realms inaccessible to man but accessible to God alone, and to things we can only perform in the power of God alone. The apostles were men like the rest, weak, cowardly, feeble, but when the Holy Spirit was given to them at Pentecost, they became witnesses who could not be gainsaid. This was not because they were men of character; they were men like the rest. A saint is not a hero, a saint is not a man endowed with strength of character raising him above other men. He is a man who knows himself to be weak and cowardly, and yet, in the power of the Spirit, undertakes things out of all proportion to his natural capacities. This is true in all fields. Faith means believing that the Spirit introduces us into fields which are inaccessible to our natural reason, but into which, enlivened by the Spirit, we can penetrate, because the power of God upholds us.

In all this we see an order of its own kind, bearing in itself its own evidence: the order of holiness. Now I have constantly said that the object of faith is the existence, in the world, of works which are the works of God, not the works of man, and that it is precisely this that constitutes the distinctive order of the Gospel, of the Church, of Christianity. That is to say that we are called to express ourselves at a level which surpasses us, but that we can only surpass ourselves insofar as that which is beyond us comes to seek us where we are, in order to raise us above ourselves. Once again, the whole of Christianity is there: man being unable to come to God, God comes to seek man, to bring us into himself. The Spirit is that uplifting power which comes to take hold of us where we are, in order to carry us up to the heights of

God. And that is the whole Christian faith. That is why it is faith, not the will, which is primary. For the claim of man to make himself God is the supreme blasphemy. God is totally inaccessible to our efforts. But we believe that this God who is inaccessible to our efforts has come to seek us, where we are, to bring us to where he is, and the whole of Christianity is there. It is the act of the Son of God, coming to find the lost sheep, coming to take us, in the depth of our misery—physical, psychological, moral—for the message of the Gospel is that he is accessible to all, coming to find us where we are, asking only one thing from us, a total trust—and that is faith —and introducing us by his Spirit, whoever and whatever we are, into his own life, by the very power which he dispenses, because he comes from God and is God.

This experience culminates in the saints, but it is that of every Christian who believes that the Spirit has been given to him and works in him. This work of the Spirit can operate on very different levels, for we are very tough material, and the Spirit has a hard task to transform us in depth. Our intellect is terribly rationalistic, our affections are terribly possessive, our will is terribly obstinate, and it takes time for the Spirit to transform us. Time, moreover, is one of the essential factors of faith. But faith consists precisely in believing that in the Spirit we are engaged in a process of transformation, in which it is enough to trust. From this point of view, the great enemy of the Spirit is impatience. Men are generally in too great a hurry, especially in the spiritual order. To be able to hold on through time, to stand up to the test of time, is the great secret in all fields. It is the secret of love, it is the secret of genius, it is the secret of holiness; nothing is real that has not stood the test of time. From the point of view of genius, it was Rilke who said: "Patience is all." (Read again his *Letters to a Young Poet*.) It is the proof of love; love is only finally verified when it has resisted time; it is only then that it descends from the superficial to zones of depth. Holiness is genuine only when it has resisted time. It means submitting to the test of time experiences which are genuine, but cannot be integrated until they have been lived in patience and in daily life. This is the experience of the life of the Spirit.

THE THEOLOGICAL EXPLANATION

Thus, as it is through the Old Testament that I know there is one God, as it is through the New Testament that I know there is a Son of God, so it is through the Church that I know there is a Spirit. So Gregory of Nazianzus was right in saying that the Church is the time of the revelation of the Spirit, that is, the time when the Spirit reveals himself through his works, in the Church and in the hearts of men. This constitutes a prior fact, that of the "existence of the Three," which is attested by the Old Testament, the New Testament, and the Church. The intellect has no concern but to know the real. It is not a question of system, or construction, or projection; it is a question of knowing reality.

It remains to consider how the Christians reflected on the implications of this gift of Revelation. What are the organic relations of the Three? Scripture does not explain this. This is where theology comes in. It is a reflection on the implications of Scripture and Tradition. It is the error of a certain biblicism to think that one can confine oneself to Scripture. We are obliged to speak from the starting point of Scripture, but we cannot confine ourselves to its formulation. There were two possibilities here. The first was to say: they are three, therefore the three represent three different degrees. There is the Father who is the supreme God, the Son who has an inferior divinity, and the Spirit who represents a still lower degree. It is the hierarchical idea, which we find in many philosophical systems and which is philosophically satisfying. There is a hierarchy of essences. It is what we find in neoplatonism and Hinduism. But on this theory it is clear that the Spirit is not God in the proper sense, and consequently, as the Fathers of the fourth century said, when the Spirit is given to us in baptism, if he is not God, he cannot make us God, and in that sense we are cheated. Here we see how it is the real which resists. By that I mean that we always try to reduce reality to categories which satisfy us, but it is reality which resists us. The definition of the Trinity, as it was given by the Council of Nicaea, is the reverse of a construction of the mind. It is an example of the way in which the real resists the mind, until the mind has expressed it correctly.

It often happens, when we are thinking, that we first make approximations, and then we feel that they do not agree with the reality. So it is the real which is always the final criterion. To think does not mean to superimpose our speculations on the real; it means to penetrate the real. And that is why the Christian sense resisted explanations for three centuries, until at the Council of Nicaea a correct explanation was reached. It said that the Three are consubstantial, that is, that they are absolutely God in the same full sense of the word, and that what distinguishes them is not different degrees of participation in the divinity. But if the Three are absolutely God in the full sense of the word, what is it that can then distinguish them?

We are here in a field which is the supreme adventure of the intellect. In all human history there is nothing greater than this adventure of the human intellect, venturing into the supreme zones of reality. To relegate faith to the domain of unverifiable options, the domain of subjectivity, is the worst treason against that optimism which Christianity professes about the intellect. For Christian optimism believes that the human intellect has been made to know reality, and to know it at all levels: the level of material reality and scientific knowledge, and the level of metaphysics, that is, of the structures of man. But beyond metaphysics, it can scan that world which Christ opens to it, the world of the very depths of reality, the depths of God, and of that element in us which plunges into those depths. There is in us a certain root which plunges into the depths of the Trinity, and we are those complex beings who exist at successive levels: an animal and biological level, an intellectual and human level, and an ultimate level in those very depths which belong to the life of God, the Trinity. And so we have the right to say that Christianity is an integral humanism, which develops man at all the levels of his experience. We must always be on our guard against all attempts to narrow the space in which our life moves. We only breathe freely if we refuse to be confined in the prison of the material and biological world, or even in the prison of the rational and psychological world, for a part of ourselves opens on those vast spaces which are those of the Trinity, and this gives rise to an unmeasurable joy of life in Christianity.

Our experience of the Trinity is, of course, poor in comparison with our experience of the other levels of our existence. It is easier to exist physically or intellectually than it is to exist "trinitarily." What often happens is that we overestimate what we find more accessible and underestimate what we find more difficult, because we are always afraid of existence, and there is a vein of superficiality in us which we find very difficult to resist. But the fact that a domain of life is not easily accessible does not mean that it is not supremely real. Nothing is more stupid than to dispute the existence of Jesus Christ just because we do not sufficiently live our lives by him. Our ordinary mode of life is a life of sinners, that is, a life of believers who judge themselves in the light of the truth. We must not dispute the reality of things just because we cannot live that reality fully. We are not saints, but that is no reason for denying that sanctity is still the real meaning of our life. It is absurd to let the convictions of our minds develop according to the fluctuations of our lives. I may find myself on the fringe of the Church in respect of intellectual or moral problems, but the Church need never for that reason cease to be the place of life, nor need Christ cease to be the place of truth. To doubt that which is, because of personal difficulties, is without real significance, if one is really honest. There is nothing more false than to let one's convictions be at the mercy of one's spiritual state. It is not because I feel Christ that Christ exists, nor is it because I don't feel Christ that Christ doesn't exist! Christ continues to exist, whether I feel him or not. It is not my sight which creates things, but if the things exist, I see them either more or less.

In those first Christian centuries, then, there was an effort to find a correct statement of the fact which is reality itself. It was essentially a matter of explaining a fact. One of the errors was to distinguish the Three by seeing degrees between them. The other danger was obviously to see in the Three only manifestations, without real consistence, of the One. It was possible to ignore the unity of God, or to ignore the Trinity of persons. The affirmation of Nicaea makes these two fundamental affirmations coincide; that there is only one God and only one divine nature, and yet in that divine nature there subsist three divine Persons, who possess that single reality in common, and are distinguished only by the relations they have with one another. In other words, nothing distinguishes the Father from the Son, they possess absolutely everything in common, except this, that the Father possesses it paternally, as origin, and the Son possesses it filially, by receiving it from the Father. The only thing, paradoxical as it is, to distinguish the persons is the relation between them. The word "father," moreover, has clearly no meaning apart from "son," nor "son" apart from "father," for these are absolutely correlative notions. So the divine persons are distinguished solely by their relationships.

The consequences of this, on the anthropological level, are immense, for, as I have already said, this is the ultimate basis for the fact that the human condition too is essentially a relation between persons. This is the proof of love, the fact that love seems to us the supreme value. It would be unthinkable for God not to be love, for if God were not love he would be deprived of what seems to us the supreme value. Now love is essentially communication between persons. God can only be love if he has, eternally, someone to love. The existence of love in God presupposes an eternal distinction of persons in God. For the hypothesis that God, being love but having nothing to love, created the world in order to have something to love, is clearly contradictory, for in that case there must have been a time when God, having nothing to love, lacked something essential. A being who lacks something essential cannot be God, for God is precisely the one who is the fullness of all good. Thus the revelation of the Trinity, far from being a sort of intellectual trick, imposed on us over and above a Christianity which could have done without it, is rather the supreme revelation to which we adhere because we are Christians, and which redounds in consequences affecting the whole of our life. In this way the mystery of the Trinity is seen to throw an incomparable light on the whole Christian life, while at the same time it is for us the very essence of the revelation of God.

CONCLUSION

I have said what I believe and why I believe it, and this discharges my conscience. I cannot endure this silence about God, to which Christians are sometimes accomplices, and I had to break it. Perhaps I shall be blamed for sometimes being too hard, particularly on atheism. I have the greatest respect for the sincerity of many atheists. But I am bound to say that today atheism often displays a sort of self-sufficiency, a sort of claim to have intelligence on its side, and this makes it necessary to restore things to their proper place and to free men's minds from certain ideological terrors. Only when the ground has been thus cleared can a true dialogue with atheism be possible.

I shall also be blamed, perhaps, for being unfair to the positive sciences. Here I must explain myself. In the first place I profoundly admire the marvelous advances of science and its technical applications. I have often said so, especially in *L'oraison problème politique*. I am convinced, moreover, that scientific circles are nowadays the most open to faith, because of the demands of accuracy, objectivity, and modesty developed by scientific research. All I have wanted to say is that science as such does not provide a method for knowing God, and that in this field the predominance of scientific knowledge is therefore a special difficulty nowadays.

On the other hand, as regards the capacity of the human intellect to know God, I think I have made myself clear. On this point I have been far more explicit than in *Dieu et nous*. If I have given the opposite impression, this is due to faulty expression, not to my thought. On the contrary, I am increasingly convinced that God has given man an intellect capable of knowing the reality, not only of the physical world, but also of the metaphysical. And if the revelation of God given to us by Jesus Christ far surpasses all that our reason could attain, that does not mean in the least that our reason cannot by itself know with certainty the existence and the attributes of God. Indeed, the whole significance of this book is based on my confidence in the fact that man is naturally religious.

The Twentieth Century Encyclopedia of Catholicism

The number of each volume indicates its place in the over-all series and not the order of publication.

Titles are subject to change.